Joy and Ease

Are You Ready to Change Your Life?

DAWN DREW

Fulton Books
Meadville, PA

Published by Fulton Books 2024

ISBN 979-8-88982-022-2 (paperback)
ISBN 979-8-88982-024-6 (hardcover)
ISBN 979-8-88982-023-9 (digital)

Printed in the United States of America

To my greatest teachers—Lizz, Laura, Garrison, and Ella

Contents

Introduction

A few years ago, I began to ask some big questions of myself, and with them came an honest evaluation of how I was living versus how I wanted to live. I worked hard and cared for my family (and many others) but felt like I couldn't *breathe*. I was tired, very, very tired, and it didn't look like there was an end in sight. There just had to be a better way! And so began a quest for a different way to live. What was it I longed for? And the answer came bubbling up from within, without thought or effort—more joy and ease. It's almost as if my inner, true self had been waiting for me to ask. "Finally!" it said. (And I excused its eye roll!)

When I began this journey, my personal life was feeling anything but easy, anything but joyful. And to be honest, it had been a long time since I could even remember being able to use those adjectives. Standing in my kitchen doing dishes one evening, I got what I call a download—a message from Spirit/the Divine/God. I suddenly had a picture in my head of my life, and it came with an inner knowing of its meaning. In my mind's eye, I saw a tiny maze, like something that you would put in a child's birthday party grab bag. The goal of this game, as you know, is to move the tiny ball from one end of the maze to the other, but *my* maze was clogged with gunk-like pond scum; think spinach that has been rotting in the bag too long until it becomes gross and mushy. My life was that maze, and all that I was praying and longing for, the love and joy, heaven was answering me, pouring it all out in a flood, but after traveling through the gunk, all that was reaching me was a tiny trickle. But love was so *determined* to reach me; it was finding the path of least resistance…the shortest, kindest, easiest way to reach me. I was overwhelmed by a love that would be so determined and fierce for me. And I wanted to know and fully receive that love, which meant clearing the blocks that kept me from it. So I began to ask questions.

What were the things that stood in my way? What beliefs, what habits, what behaviors kept me from living in alignment with joy? What kept my life at that hard, strenuous effort plane that kept me from living with ease? Was I doing this to *myself*? And if so, that meant it could be changed!

OY

N: A feeling of great pleasure and happiness

I always find it helpful to start with a definition we can all gather around as it saves a lot of time agreeing from the start what we're talking about; you can avoid a lot of confusion and miscommunication that way! When you read the above definition and think about living a life of joy, what is your reaction? Are you made a little uncomfortable? Do you dismiss it out of hand? Are you filled with longing, or do you think, *Well, that's nice but not reality*? If your initial reaction to this word and definition is discomfort accompanied by the idea that joy is rather frivolous, you wouldn't be alone.

We live in a culture that holds up Spock from *Star Trek* as the ideal. Logic. All the rest just messes things up and keeps us from making good decisions. We strive for logic and rationality. Joy isn't rational, though we try to make it so and assume it is an end product or reward. We associate it with acquisition of "stuff" or being with the "right" person. I remember the first time I felt joy bubble up without any external cause. Yup, just out of the blue! I was sitting in my car, and you know what my first impulse was? To shut it down because I didn't have a *reason* for feeling it. Most of us don't believe that joy is necessary. But then why does our heart cry out for it? And why will we accept substitutes? We are action-oriented and measure our lives in what we accomplish, *not* what brings joy. And make no mistake, joy is a dangerous emotion. Don't believe me? Think of a situation where you let yourself feel pure, open-hearted joy without putting a limit on it, you know, building in "safety" just in case. Last week, a friend shared that her house was under contract for $100,000 over asking price with a nonrefundable due diligence fee of $100,000 (which means the buyer isn't walking away without losing that money). She shared she didn't want to let herself be *too* happy, just in case. As much as we want to feel joy, we don't want to feel *too* much. Just how much joy is okay to feel? And is our need for safety and control somehow related to our capacity for joy?

As I began to speak with others, asking questions, a pattern emerged, and the same themes kept appearing. As we spoke about what we wanted our lives to be, I heard a lot of language around what we thought we *had* to do...and it was a *long* list! I remember one meeting in particular with a powerful female entrepreneur, and as she spoke, I got more and more tired. We had met to talk about her vision for the future and the growth of her business. She let me know off the bat she knew just what she needed to do and then listed all the actions she would need to take to be a success. I believe her exact words were she needed to "hop back on the bandwagon" and just get it done. And when I asked if this is what she *wanted* to do, her shoulders dropped, she let out a breath, and she replied honestly, "No."

I could relate.

EASE [ez]

NOUN: Absence of difficulty or effort
VERB: Make (something unpleasant, painful, or intense) less serious or severe

Oh, I like the sound of that! While I love a good challenge, I had an intuitive sense that somehow, I was making my life harder than it needed to be. Where was I adding more burden to myself? Where was I *creating* more work than was absolutely necessary? And the evidence was in the exhaustion I carried with me. I *woke up* exhausted, and anytime I paused in my day, I felt that same bone weariness, and all I knew to do was push through. And I did. All the time. Until it began to show up in my health.

Fear drives us,
Love leads us…

I've decided I've had enough of harsh taskmasters in my life. Instead of living from a place of fear, I wanted instead to be led by love, and joy was my clue. This meant looking at all the areas of my life that felt heavy, all the places of resentment I had been ignoring. I was going to find the other parts of myself I had buried in my compliance, making the lives of others easier. I was no longer going to go along docilely. I would take a closer look at any place where I felt inner resistance, reluctance, or where I had the message of "Well, that's just the way it is." And I was going to listen to my joy!

So this book is about my journey—what I observed, what I learned, and the different tools I developed to begin to build my life differently, one on a foundation of joy and ease. In essence, I wrote the book I needed to read. I've broken this book up into sections. We'll start with some tools in chapter 1 ("Joy and Ease and the Three Cs") and then dive in with the following:

Section 1: Our Relationship to Others: Letting Go of People-Pleasing
Section 2: Our Relationship to Self: How to Reconnect with Ourselves
Section 3: Our Relationship to Work: The Work-Earn-Deserve Paradigm

Feel free to hop around. I believe each section can stand on its own, but the order in which I've placed things is deliberate. It's the order in which I began to untangle my own life and to build on a different foundation. So if you want more joy and ease, read on, my friends.

Chapter 1
Joy and Ease and the Three Cs

We're gonna need some tools.

The Three Cs are the following:

- COURAGE
- CURIOSITY
- COMPASSION

These three are not just the best tools ever, but they're actually skill sets that we can develop along the way. Rather than thinking of them as personality traits, the truth is courage, curiosity, and compassion become a way of life as we practice them, just like muscles that strengthen when exercised. That makes them skill sets; anybody can develop them. As my firefighter son trained to run *into* fire instead of running in the opposite direction, we too train ourselves to face life with courage, curiosity, and compassion. Let's take a closer look at each one because if we want a life of joy and ease, we're going to need them!

COURAGE

Courage is not about *feeling* courageous but about making courageous choices. It is the decision and commitment to meet life head-on and meet it bravely. Why would you need courage to live with joy and ease? We *want* those things; you would think it would be simple! If you haven't discovered this yet, you will. It takes courage to leave what is familiar. We've been making the same choices, running the same programs, and listening to the same voices because they are comfortable in their familiarity. You've heard the saying, "Better the devil you know than the one you don't"? We can be miserable where we are, but the thought of change can scare us out of choosing something different. If I'm honest with you, there are many mornings I have woken up scared out of my mind after making a change, many sleepless nights I have wrestled with second-guessing myself. Change is not for the faint of heart. We both crave and dread it. It requires courage to stay the course. Remember this: Just because you're afraid doesn't mean you've made the wrong choice. It just means you've stepped out of your comfort zone. The skill set of courage helps us move toward what we want rather than avoid what we don't.

It takes courage to face ourselves honestly. It takes courage to speak truthfully to others. It takes courage to try something new and to risk failure. And honestly, it takes courage to be happy and to choose joy. It takes no effort at all to be miserable. It's the safe choice. You'll never be disappointed if you expect nothing. You'll never be let down then. To live a life full of love and joy means choosing a courageous path, one that can contain (and will at some point) heartbreak and disappointment, but also one of great reward. Courage is the only way to create a life you love; it is the only way to build within yourself the capacity to hold the life you imagine, the one you dream of. As Joseph Campbell said, "The cave you fear to enter holds the treasure you seek." It's there on the other side of what you fear. Little dreams, little life. Big dreams, big life. And the bigger the life, the more courage is required. And you deserve to live that life; you really do. And don't let anyone else determine the size or shape of your dreams. The large dream is the one YOU want, the one you dream of, and is not set by someone else. And while the aha moments are exhilarating, it takes courage to walk them out in daily practice.

The second tool we'll need on our journey follows.

URIOSITY

Curiosity is the difference between a fixed mindset and a growth mindset. If you've not heard those terms before, let me take a moment to explain what each is and why developing the right mindset will change your life and help you have more joy and ease.

Fixed mindset

Just like it sounds, this mindset is closed. Our beliefs and opinions are already formed. We have all the information we need or want; our minds are made up. New information simply bounces off us or meets with arguments and resistance. Typically, life simplifies into right/wrong, good/bad, pass/fail categories and absolutes. Its goal is to stay safe, manageable and predictable, and in control. Comfortable. Anything that comes to us that doesn't fit our already-formed beliefs is the enemy and must be destroyed, dismissed, or resisted. It doesn't budge, nor does it want to. It asks, sometimes demands, that others change, because it won't. To be fair, a fixed mindset isn't always bad. It can be the structure that brings a working order to our daily lives and a certain comfort level of safety. This is the way we do things, the way we always have done things, and the way we will continue to do things. It's helpful to have structure. The difficulty is when it becomes rigid. You can see where a fixed mindset has its limits. If you want to change and grow, this mindset is going to shut you down.

Growth mindset

This mindset is open to new ideas, open to seeing new ways of doing things, and open to changing its mind; it is willing to consider a new point of view. Those with a growth mindset trust their ability to grow, learn, and weather the discomfort of change. They understand that life isn't fixed, which instead of being terrifying is actually a source of hope and maybe even a little exciting. They don't demand the world to remain the same or to be immutable (good luck with that!) to keep their equilibrium.

In order to live a life of joy and ease, we need to be ready to see from a different perspective, take in new information, and allow our world to change and ourselves with it. Not only does that involve courage, but it requires a commitment to having a growth mindset. Curiosity invites this information with a "tell me more…" rather than walling off to maintain its viewpoint. It invites conversation and discussion. It's not threatened by new information or a challenge. It is willing to concede there are different perspectives and possibly different approaches, even if it ends up disagreeing with someone else. Curiosity allows us to drop "should" and to find a way that works for us and others. It helps us be on the same side examining a matter instead of at opposite ends of it. And curiosity allows for true healing and revelation. It leads us to find answers that really work rather than leaving us with rules or a diagnosis that doesn't. Bringing the tool of curiosity helps you to soften where you would be hard and to be open without defensiveness. As you travel on this journey, most likely you'll bump up against an area or two where you have a fixed mindset (like me with technology!). Learning how to navigate through those places into openness will change your life! Curiosity is your friend.

OMPASSION

"And the greatest of these is love" (1 Corinthians 13:13).

Many of us fear compassion—giving it to ourselves or others—because we are afraid if we give it, nothing will change. Or worse yet, we will be taken advantage of. It's true, until we get some life experience and grow wise, compassion may have us getting fooled on occasion. But the older I get, I become more convinced that the only true transformational power in the world is love. When we use shame and guilt, when we use power or force, we don't really change anything. We only cause that something to hide. And the moment we stop using those other tools, the thing we were trying to stop shows right back up again, often stronger for going underground. Nothing is really resolved. Compassion allows us to lay down enmity with whatever has been bothering us. "What we resist persists," as the saying goes. I often think of a Chinese finger trap (another kid's birthday party favor). We place our fingers in either end quite easily, but the harder we pull to get them out, the more stuck we are. Force and resistance tighten their hold. And if you don't know about Chinese finger traps, how about the seat belt that gets stuck just when you're in a hurry? The harder you pull in frustration, the more that seat belt resists you. But calm down, slow down, and it eases right out. Compassion is a great tool to use when we're stuck. I'm still learning this—how to be compassionate with myself. And when I'm able to have compassion, I release hurt and fear faster, accepting myself and others more. It's such a different experience to be seen and acknowledged with compassion! Often, just seeing with the eyes of love is enough to create change and open the way before us. No doubt it makes the process of change and growth easier. The effects of fear only last so long, but love transforms.

Compassion allows me to be happy *now*, not *when* something changes. It gives me permission to accept myself and others as is, without being perfect. And compassion should always, ALWAYS be practiced *first* with ourselves. Be generous with yourself in your compassion.

Section 1

Relationship to Others
Letting Go of People-Pleasing

Chapter 2
People-Pleasing

The Cost of Relationship

Hiding myself to keep you
Making myself smaller.

Your needs, not mine.
Overlooking slights, selfishness,
Whitewashing, believing the best version.

Bite my tongue,
Swallow my words,
Take the blame,
Shoulder the responsibility,
Understanding, excusing.

Your ego is fragile,
You do not "see," you are blind.
How can I hold you responsible?

But I have turned a corner now.
The "cost of relationship"
Is too dear a price to pay.

It costs my relationship with myself.

The Cost of Relationship
(With myself)

Be true.
Listen.
Speak up.
Release those who cannot travel with you.
Love anyway…
For that is who I am

Forgive.
Dream.
Dance.
Be weird and unusual.
Be willing to be misunderstood.
Be willing to be a mystery.
Be my own friend.
Be my devoted partner and advocate.
Acceptance.
Grace.
Love.

Author: Dawn Drew, September 2021

People-pleasing is probably one of the heaviest burdens we can carry through life; I know it's certainly been one of mine. I begin with this topic because it's the place where I began the journey into joy and ease, though I didn't know it at the time. At the end of 2018, someone in my life posed the question, "What do you want to leave behind as you enter the new year?" My answer was immediate: people-pleasing. I was so very weary of carrying the burden of how everybody felt, how everybody might perceive me, feeling like I needed to make everybody happy, so I set out into the new year with the intention to leave people-pleasing behind. Years earlier, I had a dear friend and early mentor tell me, "Dawn, you're the kind of person who will do your work and everybody else's too." And while

I was a bit offended, truth demanded I admit she was right, though I didn't see how deeply people-pleasing was woven into my life and relationships. Twenty nineteen was the year! Each time I felt the need or made the decision to people-please, I took time to ask, "What just happened here?" and to examine what was behind each instance. And what I discovered was certain clusters of behaviors and triggers. It wasn't just the umbrella of "people pleasing" that I needed to "just stop" doing as we tell ourselves. (JUST SET BOUNDARIES!) But I began to notice certain beliefs and habits that kept me in the behaviors I no longer wanted. Like well-worn grooves, I found I would just helplessly slip back into what I said I no longer was going to do! But bringing awareness to them opened up space where choice could happen. Amazing! And if you find yourself relating to this, I recommend bringing the three Cs—courage, curiosity, and compassion—as we get ready to look within.

NURTURE ['nerCHer]

Verb

1. Care for and encourage the growth or development of.
2. The practice of caring for and encouraging the growth or development of someone or something.

Very noble. Except when it becomes out of balance where we don't also receive the note that we are to nurture ourselves. When our only value and identity come from caring for and serving others, we are out of balance. It can show up as an addiction to being the hero and answer-person. Who doesn't love to be a superhero? Perhaps you are just paying the "cost of relationship," that very expensive "membership" price you pay for admittance. Whatever the reason, when you find yourself saying yes when you want to say no, you are now in people-pleasing mode.

People-pleasing is probably more prevalent among women as we've been taught culturally that this is a woman's highest calling to be nurturers. Growing up in the religious tradition as I did, this was even more expected and encouraged. I grew up with the message, "Men were made for God, women were made for men," therefore reinforcing the idea I just existed for the benefit of others, especially the men in my life. Layer onto that the message, "It is more blessed to give than to receive," and you've got a prescription for being a truly "good" person: live for others. And this is not the only place we learn to people-please. It can also develop as a result of our assigned roles in our family, having to caretake a parent or a sibling or significant other in their addiction or sickness, or through navigating their emotional land mines and woundedness.

Getting our foundations right

Around the time of beginning this journey, I became more sensitive to whether I was making choices out of love or fear. And based on that new awareness, I began to suspect that the source of my choices would affect their outcome. If you use shoddy materials, you will build a shoddy house. So if I wanted a life of more joy and ease, I needed to build *with* joy and ease, right? It stands to reason, the very things upon which we build our lives are the very things we will need to continue to do to maintain them. Does it make sense that we would be able to create a life of joy and ease by hard work and stress? I had been holding the idea that if I worked hard enough, one day, I would get to the point where I could rest. If I suffered enough and deferred fun enough, I would one day reach a point where I could have as much fun as I wanted…one day.

It seems that getting our foundation right may be pretty important. As people-pleasers, we may not be serving others as well as we think…or ourselves. If you feel lots of guilt, if you find yourself resentful or just plain exhausted, you may be carrying the burden of people-pleasing, and what you produce from that foundation will be more of the same.

Chapter 3

Beliefs and Behaviors That Keep Us in People-Pleasing

These are these are the ideas we will be developing in this chapter.

1. I have no value except what I can do for others.
2. The belief you are being selfish.
3. Being uncomfortable with someone else's discomfort.
4. The fear of letting someone else down/disappointing or hurting them.
5. Giving to get / giving to create connection with another.
6. Giving to avoid dealing with my own stuff.
7. Survival.

At the root of all these, I discovered I was way more connected to others, their thoughts and feelings and needs, than to myself. This is especially true for those of us who are highly sensitive or empathic. Finding balance was not about disconnecting from others and just slapping up a boundary. I needed to look within to see what was going on inside me and strengthen the connection to *myself* in order to make better decisions that were in alignment with my values and my calling. Otherwise, I would continue to watch life pass before my eyes while never getting to the things I valued. I often asked the question, when was it going to be *my* turn? When indeed!

Let's look at some of these common-held beliefs.

1 I have no value except what I can do for others.

My mom used to tell the story of this quote my grandmother kept on the windowsill of her childhood home. It went like this:

> I slept and dreamed that life was beauty,
> I woke to find that life was duty.

My mom *loved* that quote, and it was her guiding mantra. As a kid, it filled me even then with horror! How awful! When our identity is based on what we can do for others, our worth is always being established outside ourselves, and it's always up for grabs. My mom very colorfully told me, "One 'Ah, shit!' wipes out all the 'Attaboys'!" Our identity is narrowed down to what we can do and what we can't do for others, and as we experience changes in our lives, we grow older, our bodies can't do what they used to, we get sick or are exhausted, and we don't have the time or resources. Our "value" is diminished. This is not a great growing-old plan, or just being-human plan. And it leads us to say yes when we need to say no. While it seems we are serving others, our giving is really a way of serving ourselves. We have to give to feel alive or to justify our existence. And we can't see the strings attached to our serving, but they're there. We get mad when we're not appreciated because we have this unspoken agreement that I give, and you appreciate me, adore me, admire me. And then you OWE me (we don't talk about this or even admit we have this expectation). We don't realize this is part of the agreement until we don't feel appreciated or admired, and then we are angry and may even leave the relationship. We aren't giving out of our overflow because it makes us happy but giving out of our own need to feel valued.

We've all had the experience of giving people (often our family members or friends) jobs to do to keep them busy, and it's more work than help to us. I remember when I got married, I had to make up jobs to assign to key people so they felt important at my wedding and so their feelings didn't get hurt. Then they ended up mad at me anyway because I didn't properly appreciate all they were doing for me! (If only they knew! Why didn't I speak up?) I made the choice to take on the burden of their feelings rather than my own, and that, my friends, was people-pleasing! And the irony was none of us was happy at the end of that story! Often people-pleasing backfires on us! Brené Brown says, "Clear is kind, unclear is unkind." And as I get older, those words challenge me to become more direct and truthful with myself and others.

Needing to be needed, this form of people-pleasing places a burden on other people. In essence, we are asking them to do what only we can truly do for ourselves. Our value cannot be safely and securely established by someone or something else. It will create an out-of-balance, insecure life. And when we live this way, we don't understand what we are asking others to do for us. Yes, we want to be appreciated. Yes, we want to give our gifts. But when our identity is tied to the giving, it becomes compulsion where choice is taken away from us. We now are driven by our people-pleasing. And people will either take advantage of that (and we become resentful), or they back away from it because it doesn't feel clean, and we feel shut out or rejected. Others can feel there's a catch in there, and if they can't, they are puzzled and confused by our reactions after the fact.

Self-care is being able to say, "I simply don't have time." Regularly postponing self-care is classic when we don't value ourselves (I'll sleep when I'm dead) and a pretty clear indication you don't find yourself important just on your own, without doing. The work is more important, others are more important, and achievement is more important. If you find this sentence, "I don't have time," regularly coming out of your mouth or at least popping into your head, you may want to stop and examine yourself and beliefs around this idea. While there are times in our lives where we must "pull out all the stops," when we value ourselves, we find creative ways to care for ourselves, even in the midst of those busy seasons.

Finally, a good question to pause with is this: if I give to others in this instance, am I diminishing *them*? Many times the answer is no, but sometimes the answer is yes. The "rescue," while feeling good in the moment, is postponing someone else's need to grow. With a compulsive need to give, we may be dishonoring or diminishing another. We can't deliver people from their own work. When we are willing to look at *why* we are people-pleasing, we can actually do a better job of giving effectively to others. Being driven by our own needs blocks wisdom and intuition. Giving is not the only tool in our relational toolbox of loving others!

2 The belief you are being selfish.

This actually is a judgment against ourselves. We feel we MUST serve others, and taking time for ourselves and caring for our own needs is selfish. The equations look like this:

Serving = good
Taking care of ourselves = bad/selfish

As I mentioned earlier, as an empath and feeling-centered person, I easily and immediately connected to others—their needs, their hurts, and their expectations. But I was woefully disconnected from myself with my needs and feelings. In fact, if they surfaced at all, it was easy to dismiss their importance outright. This created the perfect foundation for my out-of-balance life in which I flirted regularly with burnout. I was so keenly aware of other people and what they were feeling but completely disconnected from what I was feeling. To live this way creates a dangerous dynamic in terms of physical health as well as in our ability to have healthy relationships. It blocks us from discerning danger and recognizing situations and/or people who are dangerous to us or toxic. And it's a common problem in the people with whom I meet. I see emotional disconnects. I see people who are disconnected from their bodies, which manifests in a variety of ways such as being unable to tell when they are full and when they are tired or in physical pain…until it reaches a crisis level. And I have observed these dynamics in myself as well. We disconnect from ourselves in order to survive when there is conflict we cannot process. Taking time to connect and know ourselves is vital for personal health and well-being. And it is necessary for a life of joy and ease.

One of the beliefs that contributes to feeling "selfish" is the belief we should not have needs. I personally have struggled with the ideal that being spiritually mature would mean I should just give and give and never need anything from anyone. To have needs was to be "weak." And to admit to having needs made me feel extremely vulnerable and even ashamed. For years, I didn't question the double standard of allowing others to have needs that I would meet while not allowing myself to have them.

Resentment is a red flag. Resentment shows up when we are doing something for others that we feel they should be doing for themselves. I began to notice as a parent instances where I was feeling resentful toward my kids, and I realized I was doing things for them that I felt they were quite capable of doing for themselves. In the past, I may have needed to do those things, but they had reached an age where they were quite capable to take on those responsibilities. They had come to expect it of me. We had built this habit of relationship together. So why didn't I speak up before I became resentful? It was easier in the short run to swallow my resentment. In speaking up for myself, I needed to set a value on myself. How I wished THEY would set a value on me! No, Mom, I'll take care of that for you. We love you so much… You are tired, and you do so much for us! We'll do the dishes / vacuum / take out the trash / clean the house… And quite frankly, it was easier to just do it myself than learn the skill of speaking up for myself and changing the status quo. Surely I could wait these little urchins out! How many more years till they leave home? But the price I was paying to remain silent was going to take its toll in Mom being an angry, resentful, passive-aggressive, snarky mom. That didn't seem like a good plan either. Honestly, this dynamic can show up just as easily in friendships and relationships with partners. Because if you do it in one relationship, you're most likely doing it in others. The short-term discomfort of having a difficult conversation, though immediately painful or uncomfortable, seems a good investment in ourselves, especially if we want to leave the burden of people-pleasing behind. Yes, we'll certainly need to utilize the tool of courage to have those conversations.

Don't be surprised if when you decide to practice speaking up, you feel like you can't get the words past your teeth, or you have difficulty even putting your thoughts into words. You've made a habit of dismissing them, stuffing them, and reasoning your way out of them. Speaking up can feel emotionally vulnerable, which, for many of us, is painful. And sometimes when we speak up, we can be gaslighted by those invested in keeping the status quo. But keep practicing. Gather up your courage! You may be pleasantly surprised. Many people don't speak up in order to keep relationships in their lives. Yes, there's a cost to speaking up, but there's a cost to remaining silent. Which one do you want to pay? For me, I knew where the one path led—more of the same. The other one, well, I felt I had at least a better chance of creating a life I enjoyed!

3 Uncomfortable with someone else's discomfort.

This was actually the easiest one to fix! How many times do we jump in before someone can answer because we can sense they are uncomfortable? Or just that we believe they are? If we can just endure for a bit, let's just say ninety seconds, which is statistically when emotions peak, we'll be on the other side. Well, shoot, I figured I could endure ninety seconds of being uncomfortable! And it certainly was better than enduring the fallout from a choice I wasn't in alignment with. Those could result in hours, days, weeks of being uncomfortable if I jumped in as I was wont to do! It was better to take my ninety seconds up front of discomfort if it avoided a bigger payment later! And when I paused, I often found that people just needed time to think and process. Me jumping in early to "deliver" them wasn't really doing anything but making more work for me! And so I began to make different choices and give myself permission to be uncomfortable for ninety seconds before opening my (big) mouth. If you can do this one small thing, you'll have made a huge change in your life! And I know you're strong enough, brave enough, and committed to yourself enough to endure this little bit of upfront discomfort to honor other people and their autonomy. Don't worry about the times you forget and jump in with your big self and old habit. Just practice. You've got this! And you'll be amazed at what you learn and what you'll discover! It will set you free! By the way, the closer the relationship, the harder this may be. As a mom of four, my kids are the hardest ones to practice on! The newer relationships are usually not as entrenched. But just keep practicing!

4 The fear of letting someone else down / disappointing or hurting them.

I gotta be honest with you. This one is really hard for me. Speaking from personal experience, I've struggled so much with people thinking I'm not "nice," that all I've done is protect an image of myself. Part of the subtle lie of this fear is that there's no one else but ME who can meet this need or that everything and everyone is depending on ME. The truth of the matter is I'm human, and last I checked, I'm not the only one on the planet! Sometimes I'm not supposed to be someone's answer, but I am to hold space for them while they find their own answers/solutions. It is simple-mindedness to think that if I don't meet a need, it won't get met. While number 3 was a pretty simple thing to change, this one is far more insidious. Often, I measure my yes on the request being just one small thing, but I'm underestimating how many other things I've got going on. I'd love to think I can meet everybody's needs (after all, I'm sooo nice!), but the truth of the matter is I need to be about the things that are in alignment with my core values, and one of those is to take care of myself. I haven't had a good feel for how to do that. What exactly IS taking care of myself? What do I need? How do I maintain my own well-being? And you know what, at some point, we just need to disengage for a while and spend time answering and exploring those questions. Our ability to love others is severely restricted and limited by our inability to love ourselves. "Love others as you love yourself" was not a command to "love others INSTEAD of yourself!"

And as I get older and hopefully wiser, I've come to realize that I can't be there effectively for someone else if it requires me to abandon myself—letting myself down, not meeting my own needs, or not giving myself the support I need. It looks like I can in the short term, but what begins to show up in my life and relationships is the very lack of support and love I am neglecting to give myself. If I want healthier relationships, I must begin with a healthier relationship to myself. But more on that later.

5 Giving to Get / Giving to Create Connection with Another

I can't acknowledge my own needs, so I'll meet yours instead. In this construct, we take on codependency. I will meet all your needs; you will meet all of mine. I get to preserve this idea of myself as a good person who has no needs, who is nothing but selfless. And often I am trying to be just that—someone with no needs. But there are so many ways this gets complicated and becomes fertile ground for confusion, misunderstanding, and resentment!

In this way of living, I don't have to figure out what I want or need because I am losing myself in what YOU want and need. And then you get to figure out what I want and need. Fair? What an exchange! I didn't realize the manipulation I was practicing in choosing this relational dynamic. I was certainly passing on the work of "me" to someone else to figure out and magically know. I was passing on the work of loving me to someone else…asking them to do something I was *unwilling* to do myself. Love me so I don't have to. I protected myself from vulnerability in not having to define and speak up about my needs. Many of us are taught we shouldn't meet our own needs because that would be "selfish" as mentioned before. It's no wonder we turn to this secondary, indirect route of trying to get our needs met.

I learned this survival technique early on. Being in relationships that were unstable, I poured into family members, propping them up in order to hopefully keep myself safe. If I could be good enough or perfect enough, my dad wouldn't get angry and go into a rage. If I could be happy enough, perhaps he would be happy. If I could love him enough, maybe he wouldn't feel the loss of those other relationships he was always talking about. I created this dynamic with another family member as well. I agree to make myself smaller so that you will feel larger and not be threatened by me. You will feel better, and then you will love me and want to spend time with me.

I carried this dynamic into my marriages. If I can love you enough and meet your needs, you will have enough to meet mine. I propped up others so they could give me crumbs. I wasn't taught that it was okay to have needs and to meet them myself.

> I am my greatest investment.
> When I invest in myself,
> I get the highest return on investment.

When this idea came into my life, it shifted something for me. I realized I was pumping a whole lot of energy into relationships where I hoped it would result in a trickle-down effect. And I could see it for the incredibly inefficient and even crazy approach it was. It would simply be more efficient to meet my own needs, invest in myself directly, and then let you be you. It seemed reasonable to expect that I would then have *more* to give, giving out of overflow rather than deficit. Like yeast being worked into bread dough, this idea needed to be worked into the various relationships of my life.

First revelation, then practice.

It's great to have a revelation—an aha moment—but if you want to live differently, you must practice the truth until it's worked through you as a part of you. The revelation often shows as an invitation in the moment of decision to make a different choice.

If you want to create connection with someone, spend time with them and create connection. And then trust the process. But by all means, make meeting your own needs a loving priority.

6 Giving to others to avoid dealing with my own stuff.

If I am uncomfortable in my own skin, it's much easier to jump into yours. In fact, the very things I see in you often reflect the hot buttons I carry around inside myself. In other words, I'm extra sensitive or aware of the things in others that I am hiding from myself and often despise in myself. Have you ever had the experience of someone giving you advice that they clearly needed to take themselves?

We think we will feel better by fixing someone else, and we constantly find other people who need fixing. Meanwhile, we don't take the action we need to change our own lives. We see what others need to do so clearly but sidestep the necessary actions and decisions we need, often not even acknowledging the need to make them. "Honey, you just need to kick that man to the curb" from the person living with an alcoholic partner. "You just need to set a value on yourself" from the mom who lets her kids walk all over her. Or how about this one: "You just gotta slow down and make time for yourself" from someone who clearly never utters the word no. I once heard it said, we say to others the words we need to hear ourselves. Why is it we can't see this tendency in ourselves? We choose busyness over quietness.

One of the most courageous choices we can make is to sit with ourselves. While feeling scary, it's actually the very thing that brings us freedom. "The truth will set you free." I believe most of us are afraid we'll discover that we're really terrible and unworthy of love after all, and so rather than face ourselves, we keep ourselves busy. This can easily and often does entwine and tangle with the other people-pleasing behaviors we practice.

When we take time to be quiet, what are the thoughts that arise?

I can't allow myself to feel... It may overwhelm me.

I'm not allowed to have needs, but I can meet yours.

If I fix you, I'll feel better about myself.

If I slow down or stop, I won't be able to get going again. I'll just give up.

What are we hiding from? What are we afraid to find if we really look at ourselves? One of the deep fears I secretly carried for years was that I was lazy, and if I stopped to rest, I wouldn't get going again. I would simply stop and become a "slug." As a woman with a very strong work ethic, I know my friends would not just be surprised but shocked to hear I carried that fear. And as long as I carried it and let it drive me, it effectively covered up stuff that was keeping me in busyness. I wasn't hiding from laziness. I was hiding from my true self, the one who didn't like her life or herself. So instead of finding someone to fix or care for, try choosing quietness. And then take any actions or make those decisions you've been putting off.

7 Survival

Ultimately, all people-pleasing behaviors are survival mechanisms we learn in early childhood. We trade pieces of ourselves to have relationship with others, key people (our parents or caretakers), in order to create stability and safety for ourselves. We do this intuitively whether we're aware of it or not. But for some of us, it becomes a matter of life and death. If you have lived with violence or with someone with a violent, raging temper, you probably feel this at a different, more visceral level. Being on the receiving end of rage as a child can feel life-threatening, and sometimes it is. Being a witness of violence in the home can trigger this same fear, whether a hand is lifted against us directly or not. The message we receive is to comply and keep the rage-aholic pacified. I remember a particular instance when my father was in a rage over something I had done—typical, stupid-kid sort of stuff. As he came after me in the force of his rage, I ran, absolutely terrified. I don't know where I thought I could go, but all I knew to do was run. And my father chased me the whole way, down the hallway, hitting me every time I was within arm's reach. I was afraid he would kill me, and it doesn't matter if he would have or not. That was my fear. And I remember, as a ten-year old girl, wetting myself because of how terrified I was. While there were only two times in my life where my father chased me in a rage, the trauma of living with his anger ran deep in my body. I adored my father. And I lived with the uncertainty of knowing what would set him off. It could be a mistake, disobedience, or it could be a sneeze that startled him. Other times, he would respond with a laugh like it was no big deal, or with understanding and grace that actually confused me. I lived in fear of his anger, and the uncertainty of it was part of the trauma. Research shows us that this trauma can be stored in the very cells of our bodies. And they can trigger our hypersensitive nervous system into feeling like we are in danger for our lives. Thus, avoiding triggering anger in others, especially if we feel they have anger issues, is a survival mechanism. This is why at times we feel like we will die if we don't people-please or that it will "kill us" to set boundaries.

If this is you, rewiring ourselves for joy and ease is a longer journey. It requires extra time and care to heal. Talk therapy and support. Avoiding angry, negative people for a season. Body therapy like Rolfing and acupuncture may help release trapped memories from our cells. Energy healers like Reiki practitioners, shamans, or prayer by gifted, compassionate people can help as well. Relearning how to be in the world takes courage and commitment to ourselves but is so doable! Reclaiming our bodies, our voices, and our choices makes all the difference.

Chapter 4
Shifting People-Pleasing
So How Do I Change?

1 Take time to be quiet / slow down for a moment. It is essential that we connect daily with ourselves...*first.*

As people-pleasers/sensitive souls, we easily connect to others. What we need to learn and strengthen is our connection to self. One of the ways I do this is to journal. Journaling has been a life-changing practice for me. I know, I know, many of us don't have the time or patience to sit down to write and process, but before you groan at the concept of journaling or dismiss it out of hand (I was advised by a friend to use a different word, so let me know if you think of a better one!), let me say this. With this practice, you are giving yourself the gift of listening to yourself. If *you* don't take the time to listen to yourself, do you think someone else should? Can they do that vital work for you, *instead* of you? Journaling slows us down, the actual act of writing, so that we can take a look at what is going on inside. I regularly have the experience that I know more than I've been letting myself realize. It's a time where I get revelation, and Spirit speaks to me, and I've come to really value this as a practice for clearing the clutter and confusion so that I can be my best self in the world. For my friends who find journaling too much a chore, there are actually apps that take dictation, so if you need to be physically active to "slow down," you can process while going for a walk and talk into the app. The point is, find a way that works for you!

Let's take a moment to remove some of the blocks to the idea of journaling.

Remember, journaling is not necessarily about *writing*; it's about slowing down and being a witness to your own life. It is a tool to access our intuitive knowing, and it is a tool for processing. Let's think outside the "rule" box for a moment. If you have resistance to the idea of sitting and writing, here are a few ideas that may help:

a. Stream writing.

Pour it out, unedited, on the page. Don't worry about punctuation, run-on sentences, grammar, or spelling. This is not an English assignment; no one is judging you. In fact, it's not for anyone else's eyes. Just keep it simple and easy. If it helps, you can set a timer and just give yourself three to five minutes and *write*. Whatever comes to mind…absolutely whatever! The idea is that you show up on a regular basis. Some days, all I would write down was a question. Those times I fell into people-pleasing mode, I would write each down, making note of what happened situationally, and then ask myself how I felt, what thoughts ran through my mind, and what fears had come up.

b. Draw pictures.

You don't have to necessarily use words. Doodle. Draw pictures. Use crayons; use colored pencils. Be creative and expressive in any way you want. They say a picture is worth a thousand words for a reason. I was given an assignment in which I was asked to draw a picture of all the different parts of myself—the caretaker, the career woman, the mystic…all the ways I show up in the world. Though my drawings were barely better than stick figures, I was surprised by what came out of me. I saw myself and my life in a different way. You may be surprised by what you discover!

Remember as people-pleasers / sensitive souls, we easily connect to others. What we need to learn and strengthen is that connection to self. I'm telling you, journaling is a fabulous way!

2 Listen and tune in to your body.

Your brain may lie to you, but your body never will. We can talk ourselves out of things, but our body is just waiting for us to listen! Before dismissing symptoms and discomfort out of hand, take a moment to listen in. In my younger days, I used to treat my body like a machine and think it was just "dumb" if it was complaining over the pace I set. I'm learning to listen because over and over again, my body knew sooner than I did when something was out of whack or I was driving myself too hard. This does not suggest you shouldn't seek medical treatment and diagnosis from a medical professional. Seek help for any concerning symptoms, but also listen within. Is there a message your body is giving you? Let me give you some examples to consider:

- *Throat and jaw.* Feeling like you have a lump in your throat because you're "swallowing your words"; grinding/gritting your teeth, biting your tongue because you're holding back words (I actually broke two teeth this past year before I got the message that I needed to speak up in a situation); regular sore throats, losing your voice / going hoarse. TMJ can show up with grinding too!
- *Shoulders/neck.* Tense, stiff, sore. You may be carrying responsibility that isn't yours to carry.
- *Lower back.* Weakness, pain, achy, bulging disks or other lower back issues. You may be feeling unsupported and not asking for what you need or speaking up.
- *Fatigue.* You're just not taking care of yourself or honoring your body or heart when you need a break. You may be overcommitting, and your body is telling you to need to rest and give yourself some quiet.

- *Upset stomach.* You're not listening to your gut. Something isn't "sitting right."

These are just to name a few. You get the idea!

When you find yourself feeling pressure to say yes instead of no, take a moment to *breathe.* Tune into your body. Where are you holding tension, stress, or pain? Your body may be telling you how you *really* feel. Eventually, you may actually begin to notice these physical symptoms for what they are—red flags—before your mind realizes it! They can tell you when you're about to choose people-pleasing *before* you do!

We need to take time to reconnect with our bodies. Most of us are rather disconnected and pay very little attention to it until it doesn't behave in the way we want.[1] To reconnect, taking time away from busyness and noise for a little bit every day is a good place to start. Walking, yoga, and dancing are all awesome, but sometimes just sitting quietly and becoming aware of our breath, while such a simple, small thing, can be just what we need to begin to come back into our bodies with awareness. We'll talk about this more in our next section.

3 Leave space around your choices.

Ah, the "power of the pause." Defer giving an answer right away and committing yourself. Take a breath, take a moment, take an hour, take a day. Instead of saying yes, say, "Let me get back to you." As people-pleasers, we have built a strong habit of giving people what they want and blowing through our own resistance or reservations. We need to build the habit of checking in with ourselves to see what *we* want. The pause helps. It provides space to make a different decision. Questions that may help are as follows:

---

[1] For more information on this topic, I recommend Dr. Gabor Maté's "When the Body Says No: Exploring the Stress-Disease Connection," and if you're a woman, anything by Dr. Christiane Northrup. She always has a section on chakras and common areas where stress shows up in the body.

Is this in alignment with my core values?

Do I *want* to do this?

Is it the right *time* to do this?

For example, if you've decided you want more time to yourself in order to get to the gym or read a book, is saying yes going to take you off track? I know, I know, it's only a little thing someone is asking, but if it is little, your no may not impact them much, but it will impact you greatly. People-pleasing feels like pressure; much of it comes from *within* us. Leaving space around our decisions helps us make better ones, not ones under duress, even if self-imposed.

4 Give yourself permission to practice.

Like any other exercise, *it may not feel good in the moment.* In fact, it will probably feel uncomfortable. It may feel awkward. And you will probably feel all the emotions that you've been avoiding by saying yes instead of "no." Guilt, shame, accusations of selfishness, and second-guessing yourself will often come up. Stick with it; give this a chance (and don't forget to journal!). You are practicing, and in that practice, you are exploring what it is YOU want. Sometimes you may make the decision you were going to make before, but now you are doing it from your inner self versus trying to please someone else. And that makes a difference. Note what works and what doesn't. And like all things we are practicing, we're learning and not going to always do it well. Give yourself some grace. Use your tool of compassion liberally and generously with yourself! We don't know what we don't know. And so in practicing learning how to connect with ourselves and what we want, we will blow it! We will get it wrong, and we'll fall into old habits. So in the midst of kicking yourself, before you pull back the blow, pause and give yourself some compassion and understanding. So you fell into an old habit, you said yes when you didn't want to. As quickly as you can, let it go. Remember, "two steps forward and one step back" is still forward motion!

5 Bring curiosity instead of judgment.

I don't think I've met a single people-pleaser who isn't hard on themselves. When we begin to listen to ourselves and make decisions based on what we want versus what others want, there can be a reaction from those around us. Of course! We've built our relationships on giving to others! So whether we have reactions ourselves or are experiencing the reactions of others, it's really helpful to bring in some curiosity. Curiosity allows us to take a step back from judgment. For ourselves, we get more answers when we ask questions than if we just pronounce something right or wrong, good or bad. When I began my year of commitment to leave people-pleasing behind, curiosity was my friend. "What just happened here?" I would ask. I observed my thoughts, feelings, and fears. I asked myself what would have helped me make a different choice. And I wrote it all down.

When dealing with the strong reactions of others, bringing the mind of a student helped me take things less personally. People's strong reactions say more about them than us. I can ask questions to understand them, but I must be aware when I'm starting to get sucked into feeling responsible for their emotions, choices, or work.

6 Give permission to *yourself.*

When I look back at my life as a chronic people-pleaser, I see I was in reality asking for permission from others. I was *waiting* for their permission. I would talk, I would explain, but what I really wanted was for someone else to tell me it was okay to choose myself. I wanted someone to love me enough to allow me to make the choices I wanted to make. But as an adult, I no longer need someone else's permission. Why was I still looking for it? The honest truth was I was afraid that without it, I would lose relationship. I needed to be "nice" instead of whole...wholly myself. So when I notice this pull, I ask myself what it is I'm asking for from someone else. And then I ask myself how I can give this to myself. This is a much kinder way to live with myself and a much kinder way to live with others.

7 Give yourself permission to feel.

This may be a bit scary at first. Let's be honest, it can be terrifying for some of us! We're used to controlling our emotions and shutting them down. After all, in order to people-please, we've disconnected from ourselves. And when we decide to shift away from pleasing others, all the anxiety we have been holding at bay has an opportunity to come up. Fear, anger, resentment, sadness, and grief are just a few of the emotions most likely hiding behind our "niceness." It may be so long since you've allowed yourself to feel these emotions you won't even have names for them, and that's okay. These feelings did not feel safe to experience the first time around, and they probably won't feel safe now. There is a fear that people won't like or love us, that we will be "too much," and that we'll lose relationships and safety if we're truthful with ourselves and others. Maybe they'll think we're crazy; maybe they'll think we're weak or negative. And then there's our fear that there will be no end to our feelings and we will be overwhelmed by them. I wish I could tell you this was an easy process. But on the other side is the good stuff. We can't shut down the difficult emotions without also shutting down all the others. The same sieve used to strain out one strains out the others. We'll talk more about this in section 2: "Relationship to Self: How to Reconnect with Ourselves."

Section 2

Relationship with Self How to Reconnect with Ourselves

How to Reconnect with Ourselves

Before we can set boundaries, before we can do *anything* that will lead to joy and ease, we need to first connect with ourselves, the deepest part of ourselves, especially the parts we've left behind. Life indeed is lived from the inside out, and to reconnect with ourselves is to be aware of those parts of us that need to be heard, acknowledged, and integrated so we may live in a way that is aligned with who we are. If we don't do this, we will forever be tossed about by the expectations of others, how the culture tells us we should live, and always feel like there must be something *more*. And what is reflected back to us from others may not be serving us. What exactly is it we need to connect with, and how do we do that? There are three key areas.

1. Our feelings or emotions
2. Our body
3. Our thoughts

Let's take a look at each one in turn.

Chapter 5

Reclaiming Our Feelings

Reclaiming our feelings

I've spent a lifetime apologizing for my feelings and being self-conscious about them. In our culture, though often unspoken, we have a bias against emotions; we are uncomfortable *with* them and *around* them. We tend to shut them down in others, and most of us have learned to shut them down within ourselves and to separate ourselves from them. We even have a range of acceptable emotions, and though difficult to quantify, we have a "cap" on them—how *much* we are allowed to feel, as well as the *duration* we are allowed to feel them. We don't? How often is the word *normal* assigned? "That's just not normal," we say. If others aren't saying it to us, listen to how we talk to ourselves. "I should be over this by now." "I don't know what's wrong with me I should...[fill in the blank]." There's an overall discomfort with emotions, and what we aren't comfortable with, we tend to ignore or try to eradicate. We have valued stoicism in our Western culture and raised it to the level of a virtue. Never complain. Saintly. Even-tempered. Selfless. Be "*nice.*" The last one, I believe, is one of the greatest choke points of emotions and to setting boundaries.

"Keep your chin up."

"Keep a stiff upper lip."

That's certainly my parent's generation, the one I grew up under. We laugh, but phrases like, "Stop your crying, or I'll give you something to cry about," were touted out as good old-fashioned, sensible parenting, and quite commonplace. Children were to be "seen and not heard." My mom, who was a compassionate soul, but equally uncomfortable with emotional expression, would tell me "just don't feel that way." There was no room for the healthy expression of emotions in my family. Emotions were private. Don't let others know your business; don't "air your dirty linens." We were taught to hide them from the world, but we didn't create space for them in our home either. Showing emotions made you appear weak and positioned you for others to take advantage of you. We needed to toughen up. My sister was shamed for showing her emotions on her face, letting others know when she was mad or upset. "What's with the mad puss?" my dad would say. "Wipe that look off your face!" was another, if we showed our reactions. I had what seemed like the unfortunate tendency of being a crier.

If I was angry, I cried.

If I was sad, I cried.

If I was scared, I cried.

If I was frustrated (you guessed it), I cried.

Any strong emotion resulted in tears. I didn't know the wisdom of tears then, nor did my parents. It wasn't till many, many years later I learned the truth. Different kinds of tears have different chemical makeups. The tears we cry with strong emotions are designed to *heal*, containing chemicals and enzymes to help us. They're actually designed to make us feel better! Well, doesn't that change everything! In teaching ourselves not to cry, we are actually preventing the channel by which we can feel better. And those unprocessed emotions are going somewhere, stored in the memory cells of our bodies over a lifetime.

As a young girl, my dad would stand my crying self directly in front of him as he sat in his chair at the kitchen table. He would stare down at me over the rim of his glasses and say to me through gritted teeth, "Stop it! Stop it! Stop it!" over and over again while I tried to seize control and put a lid on my emotions. The anger he displayed increased my distress and crying, and I remember trying so hard to shut it all down. Later, all those unprocessed emotions would erupt into painful, scarring cystic acne, anorexia, and illness and disease in my body. I divorced myself from my emotions, and in divorcing them, I divorced myself.

My generation of parenting didn't necessarily do a better job helping our kids emotionally. While my parents were of the generation to think emotions needed to be controlled and hidden, my generation believed it was our job as good parents to make sure our kids didn't have any uncomfortable emotions. We didn't want them to get their feelings hurt, we didn't want them to struggle with their self-esteem, and we didn't want them to ever feel bad. We all laugh now, but my generation of parenting started the everyone-gets-a-trophy trend. We wanted to make sure our kids felt good about themselves, but what we didn't realize is we were passing on the same problem our parents did, just coming at it from a different angle. We were uncomfortable with emotion and didn't know what to do with them. Shut them down, avoid them, push them away, expect the world to reorganize itself to make us feel better. Perhaps in not understanding how emotions contribute to our health and well-being, we short-circuited and undermined their purpose. Wisdom bringers.

Emotions are a vital part of our inner guidance system. If we don't feel and acknowledge them, we miss out on a very important part of our "knowing." How in the world do we think we can make good decisions and set good boundaries without listening to the message of our emotions? How can we have meaningful, authentic, and healthy connection to others without them? And why exactly do we disconnect from and disregard our emotions? Perhaps we'd best start by looking at some of the common beliefs and myths most of us hold about them.

Chapter 6

Common Myths about Emotions

Here are some of the most common myths we hold about and around emotions.

1 Emotions are irrational.

In a world where logic reigns, emotions are often seen as irrational. Logic is based on the things we can tangibly observe (and name). It is based on that which we can prove. The empirical method is if I can taste, touch, smell, see, or hear it, it must be real. And emotions don't fall into that category, do they? It's hard to prove emotions, but that's not really the goal. Emotions are a tool of the intuitive. Instead of using the labels rational versus irrational, I prefer the terms rational and *trans*-rational. Trans-rational means to go beyond or to surpass the rational. I think that's a far better description! Because emotions are the tool of the intuitive, they bring information that our brain is not aware of yet. How many of us have had a gut instinct or feeling we ignored to our later regret? Something felt "off," and yet we went ahead anyway, only to realize we were right all along! Our emotions are part of the early warning system and are essential in letting us know when our boundaries are being violated.

For a couple of years, I ran an Airbnb out of the front of my home, and on one occasion, we had a guest that made me a bit uncomfortable. When I sat down to explain the rules of the house, he sat down on the couch next to me and let his knee brush mine. I moved away and excused his behavior, dismissing by rationalizing he didn't realize he was doing it, unaware I was acting out of years of disconnecting from my emotions and early warning system. My young daughter on the other hand had no such compunctions. She quite freely told me that she thought he was weird and was uncomfortable with him. I listened. While he wanted a long-term stay of three months, I made the decision, though we could use the money, to not let him extend beyond his trial period of ten days. And I dreaded having to inform him of my decision, but that was illogical. It was just a conversation after all. Over the course of a few days, it became apparent that he was slowly invading my house, no longer staying in the separate Airbnb space, and he began asking me out for a drink, for dinner, for a walk, etc. He drove around the neighborhood and then asked questions about the nearby school, if it was the one my daughter attended. And the evening things came to a head was the night I had the dreaded conversation that he would not be continuing with us. We would not be extending his stay. And he lost his temper…and not in a small way! He began yelling at me, pacing restlessly back and forth, waving his arms angrily. I felt threatened, and this time, I listened. The next call was to my adult son to be present to help evict him, and let's just say this situation wasn't pretty. I made stupid mistakes, and the whole of the story is embarrassing to me as I look back. At each turn, I ignored warning bells that were sounding. When I look back with compassion on the woman I was, I see someone who dismissed her emotions as irrational because she couldn't produce "proof." And it could've ended badly. And you know what the first thing I did after we got that man out of our house? I sat my then eleven-year-old daughter down and told her she was right all along. That voice that told her our guest was "off" was spot-on! If it doesn't feel right, it isn't. We may not always understand the message of our emotions, we may not always have a "logical" reason for feeling them, but we should always stop and pay attention. The message will come if we're willing to listen and heed. And we don't need to always understand to take action or make a plan, especially when it comes to our safety. And the more we practice, the more we learn and discern.

Sometimes our emotions seem disproportionate to the situation at hand. That doesn't mean they're irrational though. We just may not be seeing the full picture and understand the message we are being given. Sometimes what is triggered is emotional history, past memories and trauma, or stored, unprocessed emotion. What parent or spouse hasn't lost their temper to only turn around and say, "I'm sorry, it's not you. I just had a tough day at work," or some other reason? We understand in those situations the emotions triggered are left over from something else and are just coming out in the moment because our bandwidth is narrower. Just like physical pain, sore spots can be triggered by actions or words that don't warrant the response in the moment. Step on my toe, ouch. Step on my broken toe, OOOOOUCH! The emotion points to something needing attention and resolution. Dismissing emotions or ignoring them as unimportant is just an invitation for them to return at a later date. Not every emotion needs to be analyzed and cataloged! Sometimes you just need a break, a breather, some fun, or a walk in nature to reset yourself. The point is, our emotions are valuable and vital for our well-being. And you can't keep out the less pleasant stuff and still leave an open channel for the "good" ones.

2 Emotions are not safe.

Well, certainly this myth is exacerbated by the belief that emotions are irrational, but this one deserves a spot of its own! Most of us have learned to hide our emotions and ultimately divorce ourselves from them because it's been unsafe to express them. We're afraid of being rejected, not liked, or "too much" for others. So often we learn this very early in our family system. Parents who are uncomfortable with their own emotions are no more comfortable with those of their children. Without the tools they need to process their own, parents may be clumsy at best, though well-meaning, when their kids express their feelings. Awkwardness, judgment, manipulation, or even anger can be some of the ways in which parents can react toward emotional kids. And frequently the behaviors, the *way* in which children are expressing themselves, become the sole focus, without consideration for the emotion that led to the behavior. The behavior is disciplined without addressing emotions present, but both are part of the event. We may be missing vital information. As parents, we cannot truly give what we ourselves do not possess, the tools and space to process feelings in a healthy, effective way.

In stressed family systems, where parental discord, family health issues, or financial uncertainty is present, children will often intuitively shut down their own needs (including emotional ones) in order to not make it worse or harder on a parent. They sense the system is already stressed and don't want to add to it. As children, we don't realize we're doing this, but we disconnect from ourselves in order to keep safe connection with the parents on whom we depend. In the midst of violent, unpredictable homes, the need for safety is even greater, the need to shut down emotions a matter of survival.

Then we go out into the world with other kids growing up the same way, equally uncomfortable with emotions, not yet mature, posturing for position and safety, and we receive the same messages from others—"Weirdo," "Crybaby." We can be mocked for any way we step out from the herd. And not just from classmates but from others in authority such as teachers. Already lacking in our home the freedom to experience and express emotions fluently and healthily, the outside world simply reinforces our beliefs about it's best not to rock the boat. We learn to hide our true selves—our doubts, our feelings, and our questions unless they are "appropriate." We look for clues from others as to what is acceptable and normal. But the outside world can't tell us who we are.

Well-meaning adults will believe they are helping us "toughen up" to survive the world outside. But it's at a cost, isn't it? The good news is we can be our own safe place. We do this by accepting our emotions, *without judgment*. And we meet them with curiosity and compassion. In doing that, we create space for them and the wisdom and information they bring. Emotions are not right or wrong; they just *are*. And if we listen, we will learn something *vital*. And as more and more of us agree to feel our feelings and learn how to process and express them in healthy ways, we normalize them. And a whole new world opens up for us as we can experience deeper connection with ourselves and others.

3 Feelings aren't important.

In an action-driven society, we've dismissed the relevance of emotions and then wonder why we have such a huge percentage of the population on antidepressants, struggling with stress management, fear, and discontent. This is not to say that medication is wrong; they can be a lifesaver! But if we want to be happy, joyful people (feel good), doesn't it make sense that we may have to take into account what's making us feel bad? The idea that it-doesn't-matter-how-you-feel-you-just-need-to-do-it-anyway is a dangerous life strategy when applied to all aspects of your life, especially if it leads you to disregard your feelings altogether. While that may work on simple things like taking out the trash on trash day whether you "feel" like it or not, not everything in our lives can be reduced down to that simple a formula. We need to bring our hearts on the journey! We are doing a whole lot of stuff we don't want to be doing and forgetting to listen to ourselves. And instead of living our own lives, we're living the life we imagine we're supposed to be living and then telling ourselves we just need to be realistic; we're expecting too much.

The more we understand how the brain works, the more we realize how important the emotional center of our brain is! It plays a significant part in all decision-making, even something as simple as setting a doctor's appointment! It's how we determine value in being able to choose one thing over another. Do we want to go to the movies, or do we want to go out to eat? Do I want to vacation in sunny Florida or go visit family in NYC? Career choices, home purchases, our feelings are influencing and at the center of our decisions, not just what we want but what we don't. As someone who has run a home staging business for sixteen years, understanding the role of emotion has been the cornerstone of my success. Reasoning *and* emotion are both factors in making those decisions. When we lean too heavily on the logic side, we may be starving the part of ourselves that makes us feel alive. We don't need to live *by* our feelings, but we do need to live *with* them. And when we acknowledge them openly, we won't be influenced by them without knowing it! Can you imagine a life

42

where you do more of what you want instead of more of what you believe you *have* to? Expectations set by others, or even within the limits of logic, can only tell us what it knows for sure. Logic has its limits. There's just too much it doesn't know. Our feelings may give us a peek "behind the curtain" of that "more" that is available to us.

Even feeling bad serves a purpose as it drives us to find answers, opening windows of creativity, inviting us to stretch our critical thinking and to *learn*. We then can make different choices. Touching the cigarette lighter in our family car as a young child (now I date myself) and the resulting burn helped me to make the decision to never do that again! It wasn't just the burn that taught me. I have remembered pain that is accompanied by an *emotion*. (By the way, this is called "learning the hard way," or so my mom tells me, since she told me not to touch it!) Strong emotion is a great teacher, unless we shut down that voice. And if we shut down that voice, it simply gets louder in order to get our attention!

Feeling bad or experiencing struggle helps us in another vital way. It is key for developing empathy. Studies are showing that our kids' brains don't develop this quality unless they are allowed to experience difficulty, frustration, disappointment, and challenging emotions. It's actually good for the development of the brain! Where would we be relationally if we couldn't connect to others without this relational bridge?

I love this example. If I tell you I just whacked my funny bone, I mean *really* hard, how many of you would cringe with me, knowing just what that feels like? That's the power of empathy. If you've never whacked your funny bone, you'll have no idea what I'm talking about. Go ahead. I'll wait. Give it a try!

4 Feelings must be controlled.

This one I have quite a bit to say over as I've really had to think through it, and I've come to this conclusion: we no more control our emotions than we control the waves of the ocean. We don't *really* control them. We stuff them, silence them, bury them, ignore them.

43

One thing we rarely do is *process* them. To process means to make time for them…to listen to them, name them, and then understand them. Once you do that, you can make decisions on what you know, not on what you don't. Believe me when I say, just because you don't acknowledge your emotions doesn't mean you're not being influenced by them! Acknowledging them may be as simple as taking a break rather than pushing through a task till you become frustrated and angry (what I call getting ahead of an emotion, like a good parent who puts their toddler down for a nap before they get overtired and have a fit). Or it may require some time and self-reflection through practices like talking with a friend or professional, journaling (which you know I'm a fan of), or some other sort of self-reflection practice. The one thing your emotion doesn't need is to be controlled. We confuse this with the idea that this is *self*-control. While we don't need to control the emotions, we do need to build muscles of self-control in the *expression* of emotions. When has it ever been a good idea to fire off that email to the coworker who ticked you off? We develop a repertoire of tools to process our emotions in ways that are not destructive to others *or* ourselves. And stronger emotion may need different tools to help us process. How do we allow for ourselves and our kids healthy emotional release? These are questions I'm asking as I parent my last child who is highly sensitive and emotional. It's her superpower really. How do I help her have space to experience and express emotions in a way that is both healthy and considerate of others? How can I help her become fluent in understanding the language of emotions? We're experimenting. While in the "red zone"—that hot, highly emotional reactive state—time to "cool off" is key. What does that look like? At home? At school? At work? Watching the words we speak is an expression of the self-control part so we don't later regret what's come out of our mouths. I'm convinced we need different tools in different situations and with different emotions. And in having different tools, if one doesn't work, we pick up another.

Toddlers generally move through their emotions quickly because they can throw themselves down on the ground and kick and howl. Not recommended for older children or adults! But if we take a lesson from our little ones, we understand that sometimes we need to move emotion through our bodies physically. My son works out a lot. I know someone else who clocks lots of miles on her bike. I remember my parents buying a punching bag for my brother. We use the term *blow off steam* for a reason. During the teenage years, my very strong-willed son got a lot of physical chores to help channel that excess energy. And I *so* appreciated the parking pad it produced! A far cry better than him punching a wall or another person, and it was better choice than turning to drugs to numb out. After physical activity, words and logic can often begin to weigh in. Here are some ideas for when you're in the red zone.

Get physical:

- Cleaning or another physical but mindless task
- Going to the gym or going for a walk or run (being in nature is also soothing)
- Vocalizing: I've gone out on my back deck (in the country) and had a good scream. I remember one time of being overwhelmed and at the end of my tether and closing myself in my home office where I threw myself down on the floor, head in my hands sobbing, saying, "I can't take it anymore! I can't take it anymore!" And the most amazing thing happened! After a few minutes of doing that, I was over it! I got up, returned upstairs to my family, and felt great! That was an eye-opener for me.

And so we courageously, curiously, and with compassion give ourselves the freedom to experiment. What works? With practice, we'll develop a whole toolbox of helpful ways to begin to process emotions.

It's important to recognize that we are responsible for how we feel, and we are responsible for how we express our emotions. It's actually a form of emotional sloppiness when we don't take responsibility for how we express ourselves around others and to them. Justifying poor behavior doesn't wash!

A recent trip to Key West really gave me the perfect metaphor to begin talking with my daughter about this concept—being emotionally responsible. On this trip, my teenage daughter and I shared a hotel room. In pretty typical teenage fashion, she left her stuff everywhere, on counters and floors, trailing water around the bathroom, outfits overflowing the suitcase to the floor, etc. And I needed to navigate around her stuff or agree to pick up after her. That's what it's like to live with or be around someone who is emotionally sloppy. We may be unaware of the way we are throwing our emotions out all over the place, expecting others to pick up after us, or even that others are picking up the pieces after we walk out of the room. No one is responsible for our emotions but us. We need to do our own processing and cleanup work. It's part of self-care.

5 Emotions are "stupid."

When this sentence comes out of your mouth, it's a sure sign you've separated yourself from your emotions. Not only does it express our rejection of emotions, but it also expresses our impatience with them. They are getting in the way; we're not enjoying the experience of them. We just want them to go away, so we reject them altogether. Maybe if you shout at them really loudly, "You're stupid," they'll listen and just evaporate. Yeah, tried that. It's not one of my recommended tools!

Emotions as part of our inner guidance system can't be stupid. But they can be inconvenient especially when our head says one thing and our emotions say something else. Or when external pressures and expectations from others go against what our inner guidance is telling us. That can be most inconvenient and even confusing! Mostly they seem "stupid" when we don't want to hear their message. When you start saying, "This is stupid," pay extra attention. What is it you don't want to recognize? What is it you don't want to feel?

We actually make moving through emotions even harder when we fight them by judging them like this. They actually stick around longer! Shaming ourselves means not only are we not processing them but in fact are adding an extra burden to our shoulders, the one of rejection. One of my kids discovered this for herself just recently.

Getting frustrated at school, she began to get teary-eyed, and instead of beating herself up for it, she decided to be compassionate with herself. "Mom, I actually felt better sooner and ended up not crying after all!" Wow, kiddo, way to teach the rest of us!

6 I should be happy all the time.

This has been a big one for me personally. As someone who grew up in a home where screaming was the norm and laughter uncommon (and dangerous because emotions could turn on a dime and you wouldn't see it coming), I developed the need to always balance out the emotions of others. I needed to be happy and positive, especially when others were not. It was my job or role in the family to stabilize those around me and my environment so that I could be safe and also make it better for others. My mom referred to me always as her little "peacemaker." I still find this tendency in myself today, to balance out the emotional landscape around me, but I'm more likely to recognize when I'm jumping into things that are not mine to carry. For years, I've made life way harder by thinking I needed to rescue others from their emotions. Because if I hold this expectation of myself that I need to be happy all the time, I'm also prone to worry if *you're* not happy all the time and then feel the need to fix it (see section 1 on people-pleasing!). When I learn to hold space for my emotions, all of them without judgment, I'm able to hold space for the emotions of others without trying to fix them either. And that, my friends, will make all the difference in laying the foundation for creating and keeping healthy boundaries. It's also a sign of respect for ourselves and others.

Another way this myth has expressed itself for me personally is with the belief that being spiritually mature would mean I could remain unruffled or untouched by difficult experiences, i.e., I would be happy all the time. These days, I aspire to be more like a Weeble. If you're unfamiliar with what a Weeble is, they were these delightfully entertaining toys manufactured by Fisher Price in the '70s and then again around 2000. Egg-shaped little people and animals, weighted in the bottom, they were advertised with the slogan "Weebles Wobble but They Don't Fall Down." You could drop them, push them, knock them over, and they would always right themselves. Instead of being happy all the time, I've determined I will be more like a Weeble. Growing more weighty with connection to myself, I find it takes less time to right myself after being knocked off-kilter.

One of my kids recently shared her experience in gaming, how she gets really worked up and frustrated. (You can substitute the idea of playing golf instead of video gaming here!) But she observed, as distressing it is to lose or get wiped out, it's way too boring to play if the game's too easy. I believe experiencing the full range of emotions is in itself a form of abundance and makes life way more interesting! Yes, even the less comfortable ones. Let's release this pressure, the one created by the belief we should be happy all the time. It's just not realistic. We are meant to experience challenges and to build capacity to hold more of life through the living of some of our most difficult circumstances. Let's not add an extra burden that we need to be happy about it. It leads us to believe we must be doing something wrong, when in fact, it's just life, especially when we choose to grow and change.

Can I make a confession? Almost every time I make a change, yes, even change I've initiated and chosen for myself, I'm miserable… and elated…and afraid. Full of faith and full of doubt. Fear, anxiety, guilt, insecurity, panic, anger, irritability, exhaustion—yup, rarely have I experienced happiness during the process of change, though it makes a showing, almost as a promise of what is to come. And when I feel all those things, I remind myself how courageous I'm being and that I will get to the other side. Courage, curiosity, and compassion allow me to be my own best cheerleader!

7 If I ignore my emotions, they'll just go away.

I had someone reach out to me recently, asking if I could rec-ommend a book to help them. When I asked what was going on, this beautiful soul explained how she was emotionally reactive, and it was beginning to affect her relationships. Tell me more, I asked. Her reply was, "I think I'm exhausted and burned out, and it shortens my fuse because I feel like I'm doing it all." The problem wasn't her emotions; the problem was she had been ignoring them until they no longer could be ignored. We often believe the emotion itself is the problem that needs to be fixed, or we dismiss our feelings altogether, believing they will go away eventually. We'll get over it. And they may go away…for a little while. We create a bit of space for ourselves, get a breather, but don't address underlying issues such as boundaries being crossed and lack of self-care. Then the emotions return, often bigger and with more force. I watched this pattern in my second marriage. We didn't share core values, but the independence I was able to create for myself through my business gave me more space and allowed me to ignore the way I felt in my relationship. I ignored the way it was affecting my health and the constant stress I felt because I could keep going…until one day I couldn't. That one day came, and I exploded spectacularly during a disagreement. In that moment, my commitment to myself kicked in, and I knew I needed to address my unhappiness. Not honoring our emotions by listening to them is like having a garbage dump in the house. We close the door and ignore the smell until the house becomes uninhabitable! At some point, we need to get rid of what's stinking.

8 What's the point? It doesn't change anything.

I actually hear this a lot when speaking with people about their past hurts. Why give this any attention when it won't change what happened? The goal was never to change the past, my friend; the goal is to process and transform it. My friend Nancy Loeffler, author of *Being with Grief,* shared that in her grief cycle, she'd often found herself in the same place, but she realized each time *she* was different. That was a powerful moment for me! As I process life's experiences, and as I process my emotions, *I* change. I have grown wiser, I have grown more compassionate, and I have lived richly! I appreciate more. I love more…myself and others. I don't need to change the past.

Because in processing it rather than letting it embitter or narrow me, *I* have changed and become *more* in ways that I truly love! I've come to believe there is a gift in all that enters my life. It may come in ways that are not apparent at first glance; it takes some "unwrapping," but oh, the gifts that have come my way unexpectedly! If we are willing to do the work to process our emotions and experiences, these things become the higher ground on which we stand tomorrow.

9 Hiding my feelings will ensure good relationships with others.

Feelings provide connection to others. Without acknowledging and embracing our emotions, there's a huge part of ourselves we are always hiding and keeping to ourselves. No wonder so many of us feel isolated and alone. Sure, we may keep people in our lives, but they don't really have relationship with us...not the real us. Those relationships, in the long run, will have us feeling more alone and isolated. Without embracing our emotions, we can't begin to resolve conflicts with others. If we don't acknowledge how we feel but instead swallow and stuff down, these things become bricks, building barriers between us and those we desire to be close to. The cost of staying in relationships where we hide our true selves (or parts of ourselves) is to abandon ourselves, as we've discussed earlier in section 1. When we risk being seen, we may lose some relationships, true, but we may have opportunity to deepen existing ones or simply make room for new ones in our lives. We think there is nothing worse than being alone, but being alone in someone's presence is a deeper alone than I've ever known on my own.

Equally when we don't share our beautiful emotions, the love, the joy, the appreciation, we also can create distance in our relationships. My dad believed in only telling his children what they did wrong so they could fix them. He didn't feel comfortable sharing his love for us through all that "sappy stuff." And we suffered for it. Trust, which is vital to the health and depth of relationships, is developed not just by being there but also in our willingness to be vulnerable. That means showing up authentically. Only then can our relationships deepen. If you want close relationships, develop an intimate relationship with yourself and your emotions, and then be willing to share that with others.

10 "I will be happy *when*..." "I will be happy *if*..."

"I will be happy *when*..." "I will be happy *if*..."

This is the belief that my happiness depends on something outside myself. And in fact, this means our happiness can be held hostage by others or by circumstances. In believing this, we have given our power away. While it seems to make perfect sense, if you live long enough, you will realize there will always be a reason to *not* be happy. This belief says, *"I will be happy when things around me change...they are the source of my unhappiness."* This is to believe the source for happiness and joy are outside of myself and entirely dependent on things in my world lining up for me. Obstacles need to be removed, and people to need to fix themselves (or let me fix them) so I can get what I want. And I want to be happy. Why won't you make me happy? Why doesn't this situation shift so I can be happy? And then other people and circumstances become either the problem to be fixed or, even more strongly, the enemy.

I used to think that if I had a certain dollar amount in my bank account, I would be happy; I would finally feel secure. And it was so interesting for me to note that when I sold my house two years ago and sold my business that same year, *I felt no different*. I had this nice little nest egg in the bank, and instead of being happy and feeling secure, I actually had *more* anxiety. I was afraid to spend the money, worrying about how I would replace it and make more. I had *new* reasons for feeling bad!

We have so many of these "conditions" on our happiness, and so we often discover that even when conditions are met, we are no happier—that in truth, the little bit of happiness we derive from them is short-lived. We get what I call a "happiness hit" and then are off to seek another one while remaining dissatisfied and ever searching for the magic bullet of happiness. We wonder what's wrong with us. Why aren't we more happy or content? That's because joy and happiness don't come from outside ourselves but are sourced from within. We choose it, we believe in it, and we give it to ourselves. And that is why it is important to reconnect with ourselves. Do yourself the kindness and choose to be happy. Do the things that bring you joy; fill your own tank. It's definitely worth it!

Chapter 7
The Gift of Uncomfortable Emotions

Our feelings are our friends. This can be hard to swallow in the midst of uncomfortable emotions. As someone who has found it difficult, and exhausting, to experience uncomfortable emotions like anger, especially after a childhood traumatized by the harmful expression of it, I can speak firsthand to the gift of acknowledging and embracing *all* emotions, not just the "nice," socially acceptable ones. Whether we want to admit it or not, those difficult ones need to have their voice inside us as well. Brené Brown in her most recent book *Atlas of the Heart* does such a great job talking about emotions and giving us language around them. I don't need to be exhaustive here, but I do want to highlight a few of these uncomfortable emotions and the gifts they can bring us, if we listen. Here are some of the things I've been learning.

Anger: The day we became friends

Just last year, I had someone let me down big-time. Their mistakes, lack of adequate preparation, and unwillingness to work a previously agreed-upon plan led to a big mess for some clients of mine, which meant it made a big mess for me. I found myself in the midst of angry clients, my credibility and ethics questioned, and as can happen, the story of the failure went further out to other clients who knew each other. I had done all I could to prevent the situation we were in and was angry because it was avoidable. I had seen the potential pitfalls and together made plan with "Abby" that would have prevented this mess happening. I was frustrated, I was angry, and I was shaken. While I have grace for mistakes, I needed to work things out with Abby in order to trust her with work in the future. I needed her to listen to me, my observations and insights; I needed her to hear my complaints and criticisms; and I needed her to recognize what went wrong so that it would not happen again. But the conversation couldn't happen because she felt I wasn't being gracious, that I was kicking her when she was down. I needed to be *more understanding*. She had a lot (and truly did) going on in her personal life and wasn't feeling physically well. And while all that was true, following the plan we had made would have created a different outcome. This was business, not a friendship event. She was being paid as a professional for her services. As a professional, I didn't owe her understanding. I owed her honesty and professional feedback.

Unfortunately, we got stuck at the point where she accused me of kicking her when she was down. I was angry and bothered by her accusation that I wasn't being "gracious." I spent a sleepless night. I fumed and questioned myself. But when I asked the question, *"Am I being ungracious?"* I got an immediate answer. "You are being gracious. *And* you are honoring yourself."

Light bulb moment. (Or as a friend says, I had an aha-in-the-kaka moment.)

And that was the day I made friends with anger. In allowing myself to be angry, I honored myself. And that didn't mean I was ungracious, unforgiving, etc. We can hold two emotions at once. Can you love someone *and* be angry with them at the same time? Just ask a parent! Of course. This is important for those of us who have rejected feeling angry, worrying it means we are unloving. But we must honor ourselves too.

Anger lets us know when a boundary has been crossed. I'm happy to share that since this experience, I'm finding it much easier to set boundaries! I was so busy trying not to be angry. I was blocking the acknowledgment I needed to set and maintain healthy ones! And so for these two reasons alone, anger is our friend. Acknowledging our anger honors ourselves; acknowledging our anger allows us to recognize our boundaries. Don't blow past your anger; don't keep it as an enemy. Make friends. What does anger have to tell you?

The Gift of Fear

Fear can protect us when something doesn't feel right or safe. I'm learning to listen to those times because my safety is important to me. The safety of my kids is important to me, and I don't need to choose "nice" when the stakes are my safety. When I found myself saying regularly to my first husband, "I'll never forgive you if something happens to one of the kids," I realized I didn't need to wait until there was a fatality to decide to leave. It wasn't long till we split. Best. Decision. Ever! I am not a naturally fearful person, so when fear rises up out of the blue for seemingly no reason, I'm finding that's the EXACT time I should give it special attention instead of reason it away.

But sometimes fear is simply a sign that I've stepped out of my comfort zone. This often feels more like anxiety and comes with an accusing voice. You're gonna fail. People are going to laugh and think you're stupid. You'll end up losing everything and living out of your car. That's when I know I've violated some keep-yourself-safe rule, I've dared greatly, and there is the system alert in my body and my thoughts that goes up like a red flare. "What are you doing?" I've developed courage throughout my life, but now I'm learning to also offer myself compassion. I can be my own best friend, speaking kindly to myself, affirming myself for being so brave. What a great gift fear brings me—a chance to love myself. Bringing compassion to my fear, I've discovered fear is soothed and goes away much faster than when I stuff it down and tell it to be quiet. And as I practice self-compassion and care, I find I have more to offer others. Yes, I'd say fear is a gift!

The Gift of Sadness

It's sometimes hard to think of sadness as a gift, but tucked away with sadness is a sweetness as it hints of something lost that was precious to us, something that had meaning and importance. Last spring, my daughter and I were tracking a little bird family whose nest had been built on the windowsill of our living room window.

Every day throughout the day, I would check on the nest. When eggs were laid, we eagerly watched to see when they would hatch. Would it be today? We searched the internet to learn more. We'd watch momma bird sit and nest, hours at a time, so patiently. Before long, she no longer flew out of the nest when we walked by. She was busy at work, keeping her eggs safe and warm. Poppa bird would sit on the windowsill, peering into our living room, checking us out even as we were checking him and his family out. What joy I had watching this whole event unfold right in front of us! The eggs hatched, and we eagerly watched their feeding rituals, fascinated by mouths of featherless baby birds opening and closing hungrily, noisily proclaiming their desire to be fed. Soon their downy feathers began to appear. We were so excited! And one day, everything was gone. The nest was empty; something had devoured our little babies. I was incredibly upset. I was filled with sorrow over the loss of our baby birds. They mattered to me. My daughter and I had connected in wonder over their presence, and they were *gone*. I was sad. I felt cheated.

Now this story doesn't sound like there was a gift here, does it? But as I processed the next few days, I began to see sadness as reaction to the loss of something valuable. And that something valuable meant that I had been given a gift. The brief time we had with our bird family brought us incredible joy. We got to see the magic of life up close. And though we didn't get to see them grow to fledglings and fly away as we would have preferred, the truth of sadness is that we got to enjoy something beautiful if ever so briefly. Sadness teaches me to hold the gift of the moments of joy even when they are brief and to savor their memory. Sadness means something *mattered*. And so each time I feel sadness, I can also let it bring sweet memories of what I treasured. With the baby birds, it was hours of joy, wonder, and excitement. Yes, it ended tragically, but the joy was real. I get to hold those memories.

When I miscarried my first pregnancy, I was emotionally devastated and had a hard time moving past the loss. Because it happened early, it wasn't a big deal to anyone but me. I was incredibly sad, made only harder by the logic that was supposed to comfort me. It wasn't "meant to be." You'll have another (really, how do you know that? I don't want another. I want *this* one). The truth was, I lost something that was so precious to me that it *hurt*. My pregnancy had meaning, if to no one else, to me. I didn't know to honor myself and my sadness in those days. I felt such pressure to get over it because others minimized its importance. Nowadays, I'm so much wiser and so much kinder to myself. I allow myself to feel loss. I honor my sadness, and with it, I more fully embrace the memories and goodness, even if that loss is only a dream or idea that didn't come to fruition. And life is the richer for it! Can you just feel how *brave* that is? For many of us, sadness can be harder to bear than anger because anger calls us to action or gives the illusion that we can *do* something. With sadness, though, our mind searches for an action we can take; we find none. It must be borne, it must be felt, and it must be alchemized. We are changed and matured by our sadness. Those of us willing to risk sadness and loss, to be vulnerable and invest in the fragility of life, experience more joy than those who protect themselves from it.

The Gift of Envy

You might be thinking, "You've got to be kidding me," but yes, even here, there is a gift if we listen in, bringing our courage, curiosity, and compassion. We are so quick to shut down some of these less "pretty" emotions that we never receive the gifts they bring. What does envy bring? Here are three.

- The recognition of *longing*. When we choose safety over our dreams, it can be painful when someone shows up who has what we want. It opens up the place of longing inside us, but when we can't dream openly, it shows up in its shadow form, envy. Envy has the ability to show us what we truly want and don't yet have. Do we have the courage to experience longing?
- Envy reveals our secret beliefs. We'll talk about this more when we discuss reconnecting with our thoughts, but envy often involves faulty, limiting beliefs. "I don't have what it takes," "Nothing good ever happens to me," "It'll

never happen for me...that other person is just lucky." These beliefs are so entrenched we don't think to question them. We don't recognize them as anything but true and reasonable, but they taste sour when we see those dreams come to reality for someone else. Being curious can help us ask the vital question, "Is this really true, what I'm telling myself?" Envy exposes our belief systems, and if we let ourselves experience it, we have the opportunity to question them. Additionally, we gain a truer picture of what is really important to us. We can make the choice to own our desires and hopes and then find the way to bring them into reality, believing what we want is achievable.

- An invitation to be happy for other people. One of the gifts that envy brings is the opportunity to choose to be happy for other people in their good fortune and success. This is something I really value! I can celebrate with them, congratulate them, and affirm them. I give them the gift of adding my joy to theirs, and we are both made more by this gift. And it gets easier with practice! Wouldn't the world be a better place if we all chose to be happy for those around us?

These are just a few of the emotions most of us would label uncomfortable. Each one brings us gifts; each one enriches and informs our lives. And I have no doubt that as you begin to reconnect to your emotions, you will discover your own gifts, perhaps different from mine or anyone else's. What will you discover?

Emotions may be uncomfortable and leave us feeling vulnerable. They may often *seem* to be inconvenient, but they are vital to a meaningful life, one of joy and ease. And when we ignore them, we make life harder. They are part of our inner guidance system, helping us know what is good and nurturing for us from what is toxic or unhealthy. They add a richness and vibrancy to our lives, deepening us and maturing us as well as deepening our connection to others through empathy and understanding, and they enable authentic connection. You want a happy life? Begin to listen to how you feel!

Chapter 8
Reconnecting with Our Physical Body

I've always had a tenuous connection to my physical body, even from my earliest memories. I don't know if this is because I'm really sensitive or not. Secretly, I've always thought of myself as "a child of the faeries." A little more connected to the other side than maybe to this physical plane. And so I've had to work on my connection to my body. I sometimes wonder if I ever fully agreed to be here. As a young child three to four years old, I was ambivalent about the need to breathe, as strange as that sounds. I would lay in my bed at night, aware I could just choose to stop breathing and pass on. I understood that meant I would die, and I felt completely at peace. It was a choice to continue to be here or not. Obviously I chose to continue, but learning to make friends with my body, appreciating it, listening to it, enjoying it, well, that has been a process and continues to be!

This may not be as bizarre as it sounds—being disconnected from one's body. In my work with others, it's actually quite common, if not to the extent that I had it. If you ever observe babies, you will see they aren't naturally connected to their bodies, but they aren't walled off from them either. They *learn* connection in that they "discover" their hands, their feet, and they put everything in their mouths in exploration. They begin to develop motor skills and wire their brains for connection to their bodies, all to take in information. They avoid food that doesn't taste good, and they don't like to wear clothes that are uncomfortable—scratchy, tight, binding. We learn to connect to our bodies and process the information that comes in through them. And it's exhausting work. Babies and young children need lots of sleep with all that learning. It is the same with teenagers, too, whether they admit it or not. So where and when does the disconnect begin to happen? And why? We take so much pride tracking the milestones of our babies, toddlers, and young children! Holding up their head, rolling over, pre-crawling, crawling, first steps, etc. Is there a point where we encourage disconnection? Is there a point this connection become *inconvenient*? We have not understood the superpowers available to us with a true connection to our body. Science is just beginning to embrace the notion of body-emotion-mind interconnectedness and the notion that each cell of our body contains *memory*. Let's talk about reasons we may be tuning out what our body has to say.

Reasons for the disconnect

1 The worship of accomplishment

The body mostly gets our attention when there's a problem that prevents us from getting things done. It's the part of us we drag around to accomplish things. We *drag* ourselves out of bed, we *drag* ourselves to work, and we *drag* ourselves to the gym. Our bodies get beaten into submission and shamed when they don't live up to our expectations. They're the focus of so much self-judgment and shaming that it's no wonder at all we become disconnected from them! We blow through tiredness, go without sleep, and "work ourselves to death," often wearing our lack of self-care as a badge of honor. Look how powerful I am; I'm superhuman. I have overcome the limiting needs of my body! I have overcome weakness, for only the weak succumb to the demands of their bodies. In the home staging industry, we used to joke that if you weren't bleeding, you weren't working hard enough! With this mindset, the body is seen only as a means to accomplish things, and it either cooperates or becomes an obstacle to overcome. A body that has problems either needs to be ignored or "fixed." Sometimes it becomes the *enemy* even.

We have been sold a bill of goods here—that our only value, our only purpose, the only way to *be* in this world is by *doing*. No, we can't listen to our bodies because that would just slow us down or get in the way of what we need to do. We talked about this briefly in the earlier section on people-pleasing and will talk about it more in the next section of the book.

If doing is the most important thing, then I can't afford to let my body slow me down. I don't dare listen to it. It doesn't matter anyway. I have stuff to do!

If we want to have value outside of what we do, maybe we need to rethink where our value comes from. Perhaps we need to just assign *ourselves* value, like we just wake up and decide for the day, "I'm valuable. Period." This worship of accomplishment takes a while to shift out of, especially in a culture that says otherwise, but we can begin to change the story. And it's up to us.

2 Judgment

Another way this disconnection is expressed is through judgment. Not just for what we can or can't do but also how we look. We are repeatedly presented with an ideal, one that can vary from culture to culture, generation to generation—size, proportion, skin color, height, weight, shape, hair type and color, eye color, breast size, etc. This is what beauty looks like. If you look like this, you have value, and if you don't, you have lesser value, maybe none at all. Not only reflected back to us from others, but we hold these judgments toward ourselves. Each time we look in the mirror and criticize ourselves, we separate ourselves a little bit more from our physical bodies. Like most, I have struggled to lovingly accept my body, struggled with body dysmorphia, and even now struggle to accept the natural process of aging, with its wrinkles and sags, its few extra pounds, worrying that they reduce my value. Thoughts pop up of, "No one will want me now," "I am less desirable." The thought that I will be dismissed out of a hand as a middle-aged white woman terrifies me. These are *my* thoughts; what are yours? What thoughts come to mind reflexively when you catch your reflection in a mirror or when you see yourself in a photograph?

Lack of body acceptance leads to more disconnection from our bodies. Of course! We distance ourselves from what we don't want and don't like. I once watched my sister call someone a fat slob at the mall when she herself was morbidly obese. I was shocked by her words. How could she call someone such a name when she herself was obese? How could she not be sad and have compassion? I now recognize the projection of her own self-loathing. This was simply the expression of her rejection and disconnection from her own body. Love embraces (connects); judgment separates (disconnects).

On my "smarter" days, I practice quiet, intentional gratitude for my body…each part. I take time to feel and center on one part at a time and tell it how much I appreciate how it serves me and how lovely it is. I send love and gratitude to that part and then move on to another. The parts where I have a harder time need extra love. I haven't found gratitude yet for the extra weight around my middle, my little sags, the loose skin on my neck, and the eye wrinkles, but I'm working on it! I see a day where I rejoice in the beauty of my physical body and have great love and compassion for the parts that need more of that love and gentleness. And while I can't see the beauty in those parts (yet), I then try going at it from other angles. I practice trusting what others see that I cannot. I receive compliments without trying to talk people out of them. I embrace that they may be seeing me more truly than I can see myself right now. I celebrate the life that my face and body represent—the bearing and nursing of four children, the wisdom in the eyes that look back at me from my reflection. I celebrate legs that have carried me miles and miles on this journey that is my life. I celebrate my strength and tell my body thank you. I tell myself the things I find beautiful. I have great hair with natural "wisdom highlights." I thank the lovely arches in my feet. Really *nothing* is too small to celebrate. These are the opportunities to love and appreciate myself. And this is something I owe *myself*. My *self*-love never needs to be up for grabs. My appreciation for myself never needs to be conditional. And in doing this for myself, I let others off the hook. I enter a world where I have filled my own cup, and I don't enter the world a beggar. I have found that when I ask others to fill my cup for me, they may fill it with stuff I don't want!

No one taught me to be thankful for my body, to glory in its complexity and diversity, and to lovingly live with its vulnerabilities and quirks. I am beginning to live differently than has been modeled to me, making the choice to practice self-love and appreciation. The interesting thing is when I do, I attract and receive more love from those around me.

3 Trauma/defense mechanism

There are many levels of trauma. At one end is physical abuse—sexual abuse, physical beatings or harm. On the other is trauma of neglect, invisibility, family stress and instability, or the experience of verbal abuse like name-calling, mocking, and shaming. It is a natural defense mechanism to distance ourselves from our bodies to survive. We check out. We tune out. And not just because of abuse or because our primary caregivers intended harm. It just happens because the pain was bigger than we could process. Our parents did their best. So we cover up without even realizing it, enduring. The result is disconnection bit by bit from our body.

My parents were screamers. They frequently lost their tempers and vented; that was their go-to parenting style, especially when we got too old to spank. And there was name-calling, which for me went particularly deep because words have always held such great power for me. And as part of my defense mechanism, I learned to tune them out, and I did that by finding ways to not be present. I lived in my imagination, I lived in books, and I disassociated from my pain. It's all I knew to do because to speak up could mean a slap or more anger at our "talking back." My childhood was ruled by upset stomachs, bowel issues, and untreated asthma attacks. While I was able to distance myself from my body, my body was still telling the story of unprocessed emotions and stress.

My mom to this day tells me and my friends how she would pray that if anyone in the house had to get sick, she would pray it would be me. I was her easy child. Yes, as a child, I realized my value to my family was in making everything easier for others around me. This also required that I distance myself from a body that was holding anger and stress. I didn't feel I could have needs. The only love I knew was for being "easy." To be "easy," I had to stuff down and ignore a lot. It sure makes it easier in the short run to separate from our physical bodies. My anorexia was an expression of this—being able to deny hunger, to live a week on diet Coke and eat only a hard-boiled egg when I was ready to pass out. Yes, that takes some extreme disconnection from our bodies. And we are often rewarded and admired for that disconnection.

4 Chronic pain

This is really a sensitive topic to even touch on. Chronic pain can cause us to disconnect even more from our bodies as part of our defense mechanism. It is my earnest hope that in our medical community, as we get smarter about treating the whole person, we will look into the mind-body-spirit connection for treatment and cure of issues causing chronic pain. I believe there are answers that don't require us to disconnect but to *lean in*, ones that allow us to be present fully. If that is a topic you wish to explore, I highly recommend two books: *The Body Keeps the Score* by Bessel Van Der Kolk, MD, and *When the Body Says No* by Dr. Gabor Maté. And if you're not necessarily a book reader (which for my sake I hope you are one!), check out the documentary on Netflix called *All the Rage: Saved by Sarno,* or get one of Dr. Sarno's books such as *Healing Back Pain: The Mind-Body Connection.*

Chapter 9

Why Connection to Our Bodies Is So Important

What gifts would it bring us to be able to own and be present in our physical bodies, and is it worth the trouble, the cost, and the hard work?

1 Pleasure

For no other reason than this, we benefit from conscious connection to our body! So much pleasure comes to us through the physical! Think of it—a great meal, a luscious glass of wine, a massage, physical touch between ones you love, hugs, holding hands with a lover or child, sweet kisses, steamy kisses, sex. What a wonder our body is! Everything from the sensation of a cool breeze on our skin as it lifts the hair off a sweaty neck, to the scent of gardenias or honeysuckle or the smell of freshly cut grass (one of my favorites), mmmm even the smell of *rain*. Seeing a smile, reading a book (or listening to it on our apps), watching sunsets and sunrises, listening to the sound of the ocean, listening to a Mozart concerto...dancing! So much pleasure when we are present in our bodies. The more we connect, the more we have to savor!

One of the things I've been doing this past year is keeping a separate journal for just this sort of thing. I sit in bed, present to my body, and I begin to appreciate what is around me—smells, sensations—taking notice. I'm trying to sit down to a meal and *savor* it, its textures, its tastes, the colors! I'm struck by how much abundance I get to experience on a day-to-day basis, if I just choose to be present in my body. And so I'm learning to reconnect so that I truly enjoy the life I'm living.

Even in the experience of weather that traditionally is no one's favorite—cold rainy days—you know the kind that chills you down to your bones where you can't get warm, there are so many gifts! The joy of arriving where I'm going after braving the elements, the bulky sweater I don't get to wear any other time of the year, oh, and let's talk about soaking in a hot tub to take the chill off! These are the gifts that come with the cold rain that I wouldn't choose for myself. But when I let myself be present, and without judgment, I receive the many gifts being present in my body offers me. I could go on and on. What staggering abundance! I don't have to wait to make my first million (or whatever figure comes to mind for you) to experience abundance. I'm right in the midst of it every day if I will stop and take notice. The word that comes to mind is *SAVOR*. This involves slowing down, not letting my mind race ahead of me in a what-needs-to-be-done or what's-next focus. I let myself experience the sensations of my body. I listen, I see, I sense. What comes to mind? What am I noticing? What can I appreciate?

The ability to have this pleasure requires just two things from me.

1. Be present.
2. Release judgment.

Being present is simply to stop for a moment, check in with ourselves, and give attention to our body. Enjoy. Savor. This is hard to do on the fly in the midst of our busy lives. Multitasking crowds out any space to be present in our bodies or to give attention to the abundance of our lives. We miss so much we could be enjoying if our only focus is what we can get done in our day. Make room for joy. Being intentional for short periods in the day, taking a break, and taking time off and away are practices that will help keep us connected and more balanced. Little practices I have incorporated in my life are as follows:

1. Set an alert on my phone to remind me to take five minutes to breathe, appreciate, and reset from my busyness. These alerts are set at regular intervals throughout my day.

2. Write in an appreciation journal. I start most days taking time to write down things that are in my life already that come to my awareness, each an expression of abundance. This requires me to be present to my body. Some days I start off my day with feeling and experiencing the different parts of my body, feeling the energy coursing through each part, seeing if I can sense it, and then sending love and thanks to those parts of my body. I practice marveling at the wonder of my physical self.

3. Exercise. Not just to get it done but to do it with intention. As much as I love listening to a podcast if I'm on the treadmill, I also make sure to walk in nature and be present to it. This grounds me physically. At the gym, I slow down motions to feel my muscles doing their work. I tune into how my body feels. Yoga, Tai Chi, and Qi Gong are all ways to help you experience and be present to your body. Running, swimming, dancing, and martial arts—try them all if you like and then decide what serves you best. Enjoy and celebrate the strength of your body. Get strong(er) in your body. Appreciate it!

4. Breath. Breath work is common in the spiritual community for its ability to bring us to a calm occupation of our bodies and to help us connect to the Divine. Even if it's just something we do for five minutes (and it's amazing how long five minutes can feel, so give yourself a break and start off slowly at one or two minutes and build up!). It makes a difference over time.

These are just a few suggestions. If none of them suit you, decide for yourself. Ask your friends what things they are doing. There are some you can do with a friend or with others and some you'll just want to do on your own. There is no right or wrong way to begin this journey. These are just tools. The goal is to reclaim your body joyfully, in love and appreciation, and to receive its gifts.

2 Part of our inner knowing system

Yes, our body is part of our inner knowing system. And the body does *not* have the ability to lie to us! Often it knows something before our logic has "evidence." Our language and expressions have developed around this. "I knew it in my gut," "It just makes me sick to my stomach" or having a lump in your throat (we don't literally have a lump in our throat). So many expressions exist that speak to our body letting us *know*. Our body speaks to us if we will listen! But if we hold the paradigm of our body as a machine, we won't believe it has wisdom to give us. We will ignore its messages, often to our detriment. We will be mystified by how it acts.

Eastern medicine has done a much better job of understanding the connections between the mind and body. The truth of the expression, "Biography becomes biology," I have seen again and again in my own life. Why does exhaustion express itself in the way it does in *my* body? Why does stress seem to kick off certain symptoms and illnesses instead of triggering others? Genetics only explains a very small part. We don't know why some genes lay dormant and others get turned on. For instance, in my family, breast cancer is rampant. In fact, as a young woman, my mom assured me I would get breast cancer like all the other women in my family. *No, thank you*! It was surprising to me to learn that only 10 percent of new breast cancer patients have a genetic predisposition. That leaves 90 percent unexplained! That has me raising questions and exploring other thoughts on the subject. Is my body giving me messages that I continue to ignore until a tipping point is reached, resulting in illness and disease? It's a great question to consider.

Over the past twenty years, I have leaned into the Eastern wisdom of chakras. I've gained valuable insight by reviewing what chakras coincide with symptoms my body is exhibiting (Google is my friend!). I also make it a practice to ask my body what it wants me to know, then see what thoughts arise around that question. I am learning the "language" of my body. For instance, if I experience vertigo (and I can rule out having a cold or some kind of congestion), I know it's my body's way of telling me my inner and outer world are out of alignment. This happens when my inner guidance is telling me one thing, but the outer world is trying to convince me of something else…and when I'm listening more to others than to myself. For whatever reason, it shows up as vertigo in my body, and I've learned to listen and take note. I'm also prone to hives and asthma when I'm stressed out and not speaking up for myself, so when these symptoms show up, I stop and take a good look at choices I'm making. The truth is, my body is so kind to signal me when I'm blowing past boundaries—physically, emotionally, intuitively. We all have this inner wisdom in our bodies. The problem is we haven't learned to pay attention because we've been told it's just one of those things, a part of aging, a part of menopause, stress, or just a part of life. So often we see the body's symptoms as a nuisance or as a problem to be fixed without realizing our bodies may be trying to *communicate* with us. "Hey, look here, I'm trying to tell you something!" What if you began to listen? What if you asked questions rather than ignore or push through symptoms?

This past year, I realized I was ignoring some neurological symptoms. Every now and then, I would wake up in the morning or in the middle of the night, and my right eye wouldn't open right away. It wasn't sticking shut; there was simply a weird *delay*, like lag time before my eye got the message to open. But it was only once in a while, and so I ignored it, figuring it was related to a traumatic brain injury I had suffered years earlier. Over the course of two years, the symptoms worsened. Instead of once in a while, it began to happen every night all throughout the night, any time I woke up. Instead of a delay, I had to physically use my hand to open my right eye. I had visited a neurologist a year earlier who just shrugged and said that in all likelihood, there was nothing they could do for me. But it was getting worse! Back to the neurologist I went, this time to a neurological ophthalmologist. An MRI ruled out a brain tumor, which was a relief, and instead I was diagnosed with a very rare condition called apraxia of the eyelid. No known cause, no known cure, no known treatment. Would I lose the ability to open my eye? Both eyes? Doctors couldn't tell me. So I went into my intuition.

"What am I afraid to see?" was the question that bubbled up when I made room for inquiry. Of all the ways my body can speak to me, this symptom was happening with my eye, my *right* eye, and not any other part. I wrote it down in my journal, "What am I afraid to see?" Weeks went by without any answer. I sat with my body some more. It's always my right eye, not my left one, I thought. The right side of my body is controlled by the left part of my brain. Well, what functions are associated with the left side of the brain? I googled. Math, logic, reasoning. Hmmmm, am I being illogical or irrational? And to that question, I got an *immediate* answer. "No," came the reply. "You have become so strong in your logic that you have become unbalanced, and that imbalance has created a paralysis." And I knew immediately what that meant for me. As a self-conscious empath, I regularly used logic to get me out of my feelings. It was the way I had learned to cope with having such strong emotions. I logic-ed my way out of them! And this meant I was not allowing myself the wisdom of my feelings. I was actually suppressing them. Over the next week, when I would wake up with anxiety or other difficult emotions, instead of talking myself out of them, I took a moment to listen, acknowledge, and thank them. And the emotions seemed to pass more quickly. And within a few days, almost all my apraxia symptoms disappeared! *Now* when the apraxia shows up, I slow down and tune into myself. What am I refusing to see?

We don't always get an immediate answer, but just asking the question opens us up to being willing to know. It leads us to cooperate with our bodies in a way that is kind, supportive, and loving. We don't need to "fight" our bodies. I'm sure you can see the advantage of this approach too!

Science is beginning to catch up. Actually, there's been a wealth of research in the last seventy-plus years published in medical journals about the mind-body connection. It is well documented how our emotions and thoughts have impact on the body's health. So why has this been largely ignored? Perhaps we're just beginning to be ready to hear it. When you think about it, it's not really surprising at all. We all start out as a single cell at conception. We are one cell that begins to divide and then divide again. Some of those cells somehow become the heart, others become the lungs, and still others become skin, muscles, nerves, and even the brain. That means each cell has all it needs—absolutely everything. Each contains *memory* as well as the ability to *store* memories. Just because a particular cell becomes your stomach instead of migrating off to become part of the brain doesn't mean it can't retain memories. It absolutely can. And it will speak to you in "gut" language instead of brain language. Medical science may come up with a name for a syndrome, and they may be able to treat it, but most are not asking about what is going on in our lives that cause us to develop symptoms and conditions. Our body is super smart. All those emotions we refuse to feel, is it possible they are being stored in the body and causing metabolic changes? Our body so kindly longs to tell us truth we may be missing or suppressing. Learning and listening to the language of our bodies is vital to our well-being. Your brain may lie to you, but the body simply can't. Let's reconnect to our physical bodies with curiosity and compassion to see what treasures of knowledge and wisdom they have for us!

Chapter 10
Connecting with Our Thoughts

Connecting with Our Thoughts

Conservative estimates are that we think, on average, sixty thousand thoughts a day. How many of these are we truly aware of? It's not that we're not thinking; it's that we aren't taking notice of our thoughts! We inherit ways of thinking from our families and culture, we are influenced by the people around us, and then we develop reflexive thoughts patterns and thought habits that are shaping our days. These habitual thoughts create and reinforce our beliefs and then create and reinforce our experiences. When we have an experience, we see it through the lens of our preexisting beliefs, therefore reinforcing them. This makes it difficult to change our lives or ourselves unless we bring in some kind of awareness practice. So often what we think is logic is just logical given a certain set of beliefs, but when our beliefs change, what was oh, so logical before becomes *illogical*. That's when change can happen!

I remember some of the earliest "aha" moments of becoming aware of my thoughts. I was in a particularly stressful time, and I found myself thinking and saying all the time, "I am so overwhelmed." Over and over again, I would tell myself I am so overwhelmed. Boy, I am really overwhelmed until this little voice popped into my head to interrupt.

Are you?

Huh.

I dunno, *am* I?

To be overwhelmed is to be unable to function. To be pushed back, overrun, and *defeated*. I was still going. I was still functioning. I just *felt* overwhelmed. Clearly I wasn't overwhelmed. I just *felt* overwhelmed. That changed everything for me! I could let myself feel the feeling, but from then on out, my language changed. Saying I *felt* overwhelmed was different from *being* overwhelmed, and that allowed me the distance to make good decisions and put one foot in front of the other, knowing that I wouldn't always feel this way and that I was strong enough to make it through.

From time to time, I had other moments where that little voice would rise up within me. I remember standing outside my kitchen and experiencing some back pain—aching, burning, tightness…miserable! And I remember, in my detachment from my body, feeling how much my back hurt and saying to it, "Well, *that's* stupid!" I actually thought my back was "stupid" for being in pain (talk about being disconnected from my body!). This was actually the way my family thought and spoke about their bodies, "Stupid this, stupid that." I had never thought to question it. I just dismissed my body and called it stupid. The voice rose up again. Why is your body stupid for being in pain? It had never occurred to me to think a different thought! Now it would be much later before I began to change my practice of pushing past pain to get things done and still later yet before beginning to ask my body what it was trying to tell me, but I never called pain in my body stupid ever again.

This is what happens when we begin to reconnect with our thoughts in *awareness*. It's not about trying to stop thoughts; it's about becoming aware that we are thinking them. It is the practice of mindfulness, noticing our thoughts, and without judgment where we pronounce them good or bad. When we judge our thoughts, we'll have a tendency to hide them even from ourselves, and what remains hidden not only remains unchanged but can drive and influence us from the hidden places. If we courageously look at and admit our thoughts, even the ones we don't want to admit we have because they're not "nice," an amazing thing happens. We open up choices for ourselves without manipulation, without hiding, without the use of guilt and shame.

The truth will set you free!

> Yes, the truth can hurt…but only for a little while.
> The truth heals too…*always*.
> And best yet is the promise…the truth will set you *free*!

Are you ready to take a closer look at your thoughts? Let's look at some simple truths.

1 Thoughts become reality: the stories we tell ourselves.

There are things that we tell ourselves over and over again (thoughts we think), not realizing we are creating a reality for ourselves. Some of these narratives are ones we inherit; others are self-inflicted. In my family, for instance, my dad told us the story how things would be harder for us because we were Garrisons (our last name). My dad truly believed that life would be harder for us. He told us bad things would happen to us, people wouldn't like us or would be out to "get us," and then gave examples from his own life how people had treated him unjustly. These kinds of stories often arise when we are hurt or frustrated, and instead of feeling our feelings, we make pronouncements and rules to make sense of the world. Maybe we can protect ourselves from it happening again if we don't have expectations. We generalize and make a rule for ourselves and the world. I have a front-row seat with my teenager as we talk about these same topics. "I always make stupid mistakes" or "Nobody understands me. No one wants to be my friend," or "Things never work out for me," etc. Those nevers and always, they're major red flags of stories we're telling ourselves! And we sure can tell those stories convincingly and with lots of proof to justify them, and we'll have others believing those stories with us, reinforcing them still more. Over time, these stories strengthen. We are wiring our brains each time we say them, think them, and leave them unchallenged. When the moment of conflict passes, when the emotional triggers settle down, we don't realize that we have created a story for ourselves that will be easier to return to next time. We are forming thought habits. Those thought habits become roads, and those roads become highways we race down in our lives. It takes work to create new footpaths that become roads that eventually become highways. It takes intention.

There are other stories we inherit from our culture or the popular worldview. I love people like Jack LaLanne, the fitness guru, who challenged our beliefs around growing old. We had been told what to expect, loss of function, loss of muscle tone, shrinkage, and more, and that was exactly the norm of aging we saw in our country! Jack challenged the accepted beliefs and then changed them for the rest of us! How many of us today own a gym membership? Working out as a part of aging well is an accepted belief now.

I grew up with the belief in the six-minute mile. I was told as a child that humanity had reached its physical peak with that record and running faster was impossible. Well, someone forgot to tell the person who broke that record and all those who have since! The record now stands at 3 minutes and 43.13 seconds. Wow.

Sometimes these cultural stories show up when we decide to choose something different for ourselves from the norm. Those around you will speak words of warning, cautioning you that what you're attempting won't work or will lead to disaster. We're not talking about jumping off a cliff without a bungee cord or parachute. We're talking about maybe pursuing a different career, going back to school, or *not* going to college when that's what everyone else does. It is also leaving the safety of a relationship and facing being alone rather than live where you are unhappy and unfulfilled. Heck, even *saying* you want to live a fulfilling life can invite criticism! Why aren't you satisfied with what is? Everybody feels that way. It's normal. Don't look for more. Wanting to be happy is just "selfish"!

Make it a point to question the thought habits and beliefs you inherit from others, whether from your family, your friends, the media, or the culture. If you're frustrated and fighting against a belief, it may be one that deep down inside you don't agree with. If you resent, resist, and rail against a belief, it's probably a good place to start asking some questions! Here's one of my own that popped up the other day: money is hard to come by.

All through my childhood, I heard, "Money doesn't grow on trees!" It would be angrily exclaimed along with "What am I, made of money?" when lights were left on, doors weren't shut tightly, or some other such. I get it, it was wasteful, and as a kid, I wasn't always tuned into things like that (I am a parent now myself). But embedded into these frustrated declarations was a mindset of scarcity. My parents worked hard for their money, they sacrificed for it, and it was "easy come, easier gone." Frequently said was, "Just about the time I get two nickels to rub together, someone comes along and takes a dime."

One morning, as I stepped out of bed, a crazy thought popped into my mind. "What if you decided that money was *easy* to come by?" I could certainly tell stories about how hard I worked, being underpaid, money that I was cheated out of, and all other sorts of scarcity stories. But if I chose to think the thought that money was easy to come by, what would I begin to notice? What opportunities had I been dismissing because I decided money was hard to come by? So I decided to change my story. Truth be told, I've always been good at making money and finding resources. I was always creative in finding deals or making them, so I had a foundation for believing that money was in fact easy to come by. How much more would this grow if I no longer had the limiting belief that money was hard to come by? It certainly would be much more fun (and more joyful) to begin cataloging all the ways that money comes easily to me. Like the text I got the next day that I was receiving a bonus check and to expect it to show up in the next couple of weeks. Or it could be the new design client I picked up who was referred to me. How about the two consultations I booked the very same day as the new design client. Not to mention my mechanic who took longer than expected to do the maintenance check on my car and waived payment for his time and work. Then there was the person who wanted to pay me for pet sitting that I *almost* said, "No, you don't have to pay me." Had I been turning money away because I needed to create and enforce the story that money was hard to come by? I gotta tell you, it started me thinking! How often I discounted my services because of this belief. If money is hard to come by, I didn't want to burden people by paying full price for my services. I didn't want to take their "hard-earned money." Too often I was giving my time away.

The stories we continue to tell ourselves build and connect to other stories until they are firmly entrenched in quite a tangle. I saw this after getting really angry with my kid who hurled something I had just bought her. She was frustrated and lashed out, and while it was disrespectful of my gift, it triggered something in me—my scarcity message. Sacrifice. Hiding behind my anger was a belief that buying something for her meant that I *couldn't* buy something for myself. Because money was hard to come by. And it simply wasn't true. But the story still *felt* real to me and held me in its grip, except I was committed to changing it. Situations like these come up so we can practice a different story. The triggers show us where we may have thoughts that aren't serving us. And when we don't take notice of them, when we allow our thoughts to drive us without questioning them, they create a life we never intended or wanted. We'll ask ourselves, How did we get here? Our thoughts paved the way.

2 Choose your focus: Where attention goes, energy flows.

Probably one of the biggest "aha" moments happened while parenting my youngest child. It was one of those frustrating scenarios most parent will experience during their parenting years—bedtime meltdowns (I believe I just got a sympathetic shudder from my other parents out there reading this)! It was a typical night. We started the bedtime routine, and Ella began to melt down because she didn't *want* to go to bed. I was feeling extra pressure to get her there because the next day was her class trip to the zoo. Lots of sun, lots of walking, and a big drive each way meant a long day for her, and without good sleep, she would be prone to a meltdown at the zoo or on the ride home. I knew my sensitive child. She needed to get to bed, or she was in danger of overwhelm the next day, and it wouldn't be fun for her OR her teachers and parent chaperones. I *really* needed her to get to bed. And there was no reasoning with her. All she knew at that present moment was she didn't want to go to bed. The thought of it was making her incredibly unhappy, and it was all she could see. I had a moment of inspiration. I can still see us standing in my master bathroom that night.

"Ella, close your eyes."

"Why?"

"Just close your eyes," I said. She closed her eyes.

"Now I want you to think about going to bed right now. Think that thought." I gave her a moment. "How do you feel?" And she began to cry and to complain (whine, really). I could tell she was quite unhappy. "Okay, now I want you to think about the zoo. What will your day be like at the zoo? What will you see? What will your friends see?" And a smile came over her face. "How do you feel?"

"Good," she replied.

"Okay, you can think about going to bed, or you can think about going to the zoo tomorrow. Both of these thoughts are true. One thought makes you miserable. The other makes you happy. You get to choose. Do you want to be miserable right now, or do you want to be happy? It's up to you."

I'm not sure my daughter remembers that moment, but I sure do! It's not that we can't ever think about something that is painful or hard, but it is our choice how often and long we spend on those thoughts. If I think thoughts that make me happy and support me, why would I spend time on the ones that make me miserable and weigh me down? I'm aware that in this present moment, many of my problems don't exist. They're simply not with me right now, unless I bring them in with me. Often, if I will leave them alone, the solutions pop up rather unexpectedly, and without the worry and misery I create by perseverating. That is what I call the "dryer syndrome," over and over and around and around, thinking and worrying. Meanwhile, I could have enjoyed the present moment. I have never, ever solved a problem by worrying about it or fearing it. Never. But I *do* get answers from the place of peace. Worrying is *not* problem-solving. It is work that gives the illusion of making headway, like "busy work." It accomplishes nothing. And it impedes the creative process of finding solutions. It's using imagination *against* us.

I've spent so much time being unhappy in my life due to focusing on the wrong things, what I don't have versus what I have, who loves me instead of who has disappointed me. Choosing our focus is what allows us to be in gratitude and appreciation. This is the beginning of shifting and changing our lives. Choosing joy is often a matter of simply changing focus. And it takes some serious effort in the beginning. It takes discipline. But if you want a life with more joy and ease, that means putting in the work of choosing and holding your focus.

I recently met with a friend who lost her son several years ago. The grief is still fresh; so much sorrow and huge life changes are still being survived and processed. She hasn't found her way through yet. Her foundations were washed away. Beliefs and old paradigms cannot answer what life has brought her. At those times, life narrows down to just trying to live through the next moment. Taking life as a whole is simply too much. I get it. I've had those seasons where I've been "undone." All that I had known had been wiped away or turned on its head, and I didn't recognize the world in which I found myself. I didn't *begin* to know how to take the next step. The message of "choose your focus" is *not* the right one for someone in that place. It is unkind and given out of season. We should *never* give this message or advice to another; parenting may be the only exception here. We cannot step into the sacred spaces of another's life to tell them how to live or how to feel, and we certainly shouldn't be doing it without invitation. To utter words like these can short-circuit someone's process, shutting them down, and increase the burden of the work they are doing. The message of choose your focus will come from within. You'll know it's the right time because choice opens up for you. You'll know in a specific moment that you can choose to let it go to make another choice, even if it's just for this one moment.

I remember one decision point for me after my first marriage ended. I would keep my friends entertained with story after story of what was going on in my situation. It was all I talked about. The crazy abounded, according to me! But one day, I realized that I didn't want to be talking about this negative stuff for the rest of my life. While I love entertaining people and making them laugh, I didn't want to do it by telling stories about someone else's "stupidity" or even drama; it wasn't where I wanted to keep my focus. I was surprised by how hard it was to resist "entertaining" my friends in this way. I had spent so much time telling those stories I didn't know *what* to talk about without them. I had nothing to say. And I spent months staying in the background (not easy for me as I love an audience!), listening to others and resisting telling stories that would come to mind. Oh, and they were *good* stories. I'd start one, only to say, "Never mind," and stop right in the midst of it. It felt awkward and clumsy, but something had opened up where I knew I had a choice to choose something different for myself. And I did.

This way is not always easy, but it gets easier over time Over the years, I'm delighted by the foundation of new thought habits I have laid with those early, brave choices to change. Each new area of choice that opens up, I am willing to feel the pain I've been protecting and nurturing with old thought habits. I sometimes grumble and complain about the path before me, the work I am doing instead of someone else changing. But oh, how much joy I have access to that I didn't have five years ago, ten years ago, and longer! How much easier life is without carrying the burden of thoughts that weigh me down instead of raise me up. Courage, curiosity, and compassion have become my friends. I continue to experiment with what can happen when I am willing to choose my focus and change my thoughts about myself, others, and the world in which I live.

3 The importance of forgiveness

"The unforgiving mind is full of fear, and offers love no room to be itself, no place where it can spread its wings in peace and soar above the turmoil of the world" (A Course in Miracles Lesson #121).

Coming from a home where there was so much bitterness, where we kept track of every slight and quickly took offense, I knew very little about true forgiveness. I've had to learn as I go, often confusing forgiveness with its substitutes. And I've made a lot of mistakes to learn its ways and expressions, and of course, I'm still learning. I *do* know it's opposite, though, and I recognize its fruits. So I've had a reference point from which to learn about this precious gift that we give ourselves and the world. Without a doubt, the practice of forgiveness is central to a life of joy and ease, especially when we talk about the thoughts we choose to think. First, let's clarify a couple of things.

These are what forgiveness is *not:*

1. Whitewashing in any form

    Whitewashing is the practice of dressing up something to disguise what's underneath in order to feel better, make another feel better, or avoid conflict. I will not play pretend by calling something what it is *not*. I can hold loosely another's intentions because I don't always know the motives of another, but I will not diminish or disrespect my pain or discomfort because someone didn't mean to do what they did. I don't always know what they meant or didn't, and it's almost beside the point. I will feel my emotions so I can get past them. I will not make excuses for someone's behavior or try to twist something that was hurtful into something positive. That helps no one.

    My mom used to tell us kids two things when my dad would scream at us. One, "Your dad isn't yelling. He's just hard of hearing." And two, "It's not that your dad doesn't love you. If he has one fault, he loves *too* much." And there began the twisting of love in my life. I became a really good whitewasher too. I'm not interested in dressing things up (unless it's your house!). I'm interested in truth and then moving on. You can't fix what you don't acknowledge.

2. Ignoring, hiding, sweeping it under the rug

We don't like the messy in our culture. We aren't comfortable with pain or emotion either. We don't like to talk about uncomfortable subjects, and so instead, we wall things up and just refuse to talk or even think about them. If we just keep moving on and moving away, we somehow believe *that's* forgiveness. Out of sight is *not* necessarily out of mind. The metaphor we used earlier about taking a room in your house to dump your garbage is a good one. At some point, it begins to stink, and that stink left unaddressed will make the home uninhabitable. You *can* get used to a lot of stink, but even if *you* get used to it, it will limit the number of people who want to live there with you.

3. An emotion

Forgiveness is not an emotion, though it affects our emotions, heightening or soothing them. I cannot nor should I try to manipulate my emotions to bring about a *feeling* of forgiveness. In my experience, that just leads me to whitewash or "sweep under the rug." Remember, emotions are a part of our early-warning system, so if we begin to manipulate our emotions, we short-circuit their message and leave ourselves vulnerable. When there is pain, hurt, betrayal, wrongdoing, broken promises, and unmet expectations, there will be emotions with it. Just like when you break your foot, it hurts, and it hurts a lot and often for a long time. Even the healing process can hurt. And then it may be sensitive for a while, even after the break heals. Walking too long or too far, perhaps the weather or some such may trigger pain or discomfort anew, but the pain doesn't mean that your foot is still broken. Healing continues. Additionally, the occasional pain brings opportunities to us. It can trigger self-care, *or* it can trigger "stories," like, "My life is over," "This will never heal," "Poor me."

This is the part I want to talk about as we talk about choosing our thoughts.

Forgiveness: Letting Go to Make Room for Something Better

"[The unforgiving mind] does not ask because it thinks it knows, it does not question, certain it is right" (A Course in Miracles Lesson #121).

While unforgiveness rests in its "right-ness," forgiveness is the act of letting go, believing there is another story available to us. It is an expression of ultimate trust and hope. We release that which no longer serves us well in order to embrace that which does. We exercise our choice to release the limitations of our unforgiving stories and beliefs, in order to embrace the unlimited possibilities of something new and I believe better. It's certainly better than our stories of unforgiveness. They are making us miserable. We release to move on. And while this sounds simplistic, the practice is rarely easy.

What you hold on to is holding on to you.

In this way, forgiveness has very little to do with another person, and all about you. Each time we rehearse a story, pronounce judgment, or hold a grudge, we tie ourselves to those thoughts, stories, and even people, limiting *ourselves*. We bring them forward again and again into our present moment and then project them into our future. "You ruined my life," "I'll never get over this," "You've taken the best years of my life." Without forgiveness, we *never* move on from them. We build our lives around these stories and pronouncements, certain we've got it right. And we often make monuments to them and build our identities around them. Others are free to go about their lives, but we are stuck right here. Comfortable in our "right-ness" and our stories, not realizing how we're being changed them, and not in a good way. We end up hurting ourselves and those around us. We justify our beliefs with irrefutable proof, evidence of why we feel and think the way we do. Whatever we tie ourselves to ends up collecting other evidence or debris in our lives, tangling and reinforcing and complicating the original thought or belief. It can create quite the tangle!

I love this broad definition of forgiveness—letting go of what does not serve us to receive something better in its place because its application is broad too. Letting go of questions that will never be answered is a form of forgiveness. "Why did they do what they did?" "Why won't they love me?" Sometimes these questions have no answers, or at least ones that make sense. And sometimes in releasing these questions, the answers come later. Either way, I'm saving myself hours, days, or even years trying to answer something I simply can't. Let it go. I can spend my time better and with thoughts that support me.

Every day I get to practice forgiveness in the small stuff. Driving on the road and someone cuts me off or runs me off the road or (my pet peeve) won't make room for me to merge. Ugh! I can let it affect me for the moment—the wash of adrenaline, the anger at the other driver—or I can let it affect me for HOURS, retelling the story to everyone I meet along the way. Is that really how I want to spend my day? I've decided I don't. And I realize that the choice is mine. I can feel my emotions, have a little "bump" in my day, and then move on. I like that I'm getting pretty quick at these little annoyances. They are my opportunities to practice the power of choice.

But let's be honest, there are the big things that come, the ones that leave us struggling to breathe and knock us to our knees. These are not quick moments where we say, "Just let go." We must grieve. We have emotions to be processed and often paradigms that are being shifted. The world has changed for us. This is the work of breaking open, and it is not quick work if we do it well. The work of forgiveness is broad.

—Letting go of what we thought we'd have
—Letting go of dreams
—Letting go of what we deserved
—Letting go of relationships that can no longer continue
—Letting go of our idea of ourselves or others
—Letting go of the way things *should* be

These are just to name a few. But in the letting go, we create room for something else to emerge. While we hold on, nothing else can come to us; there is no space for it. Anything "new" will simply get twisted till it fits the old mold or old story. We keep recreating the old scenario, unable to move on at all.

Forgiveness allows us to receive the gift hidden in all situations, with all people. It creates space for something new. If you want to hang on to the old stuff, you can, but until you let go or are willing to let go, you'll never have space for a new story to emerge, one of joy and ease.

4 Self-talk

Most of us don't speak nicely to ourselves.

I cringe when I hear my mom call herself "dummy" or "lazy bones" or when she tells herself that she just needs a "swift kick in the ass" to get herself going. Why would you talk to yourself that way when you wouldn't to another? I don't care if you're doing it jokingly or "affectionately." It's just not kind. Words have power. Our brain (and body and heart) are listening and can't tell the difference between when we're "joking" and when we're not. Think of words laying down highways in our brains, called neuropathways. The more often you repeat them, the stronger those neuropathways of connection. Pretty soon, it doesn't matter what your motivation was—humor or frustration—the words now are lodged in your head, a habit of thought and speech. They simply get easier and easier to repeat; they become automatic, a loop. They become a track running in the background of our lives that gets triggered when we're angry, frustrated, afraid, or feel shame. Unless we begin to question them.

Kindness begins with ourselves.

I remember sitting at my kitchen table with my dad after becoming a mom myself. My oldest was a little over a year at the time, happily playing on her own for a few precious moments, so Dad was giving parenting advice as well as sharing one of his core parenting philosophies. "It was my job to keep you down, to make sure you didn't think too highly of yourself." Wham. My immediate reaction was, "Oh my gosh, you did it *on purpose!*" My dad believed in pointing out flaws, telling us what we were doing wrong so that we could fix ourselves and our behaviors. He didn't believe in "attaboys." Don't screw up. Mom always told us how he would speak proudly of us to others, just like his father did with him, but Dad never said any of those things to us. He didn't want us to think too highly of ourselves. I wonder what he thought would happen if he did? His belief he was protecting us by keeping us down and grounded and his unwillingness to praise or celebrate us was unfortunate for all of us. And no doubt it tangled with his story that whatever he loved was taken away from him. It was just too risky to be kind.

When we grow up in households that withhold love, approval, praise, and affection in exchange for performance and/or compliance, or when those things are given inconsistently on the basis of seeming whimsy, we tend to withhold these same things from ourselves. We can do better. My parents didn't learn to love themselves in this way either. I totally understand! But today, *today* can be different for me because I can give each of these things to myself.

Kindness is one way compassion expresses itself.

- Commit to kindness for yourself. Use kind words, kind actions, emotional support, and understanding. Start where you know to start, and this will begin to spread out in your life. Listen to how you talk to yourself and how you think about yourself. Can you hear yourself? Would you want to be caught on tape saying or thinking this stuff? Then maybe you best choose something kinder.
- Kindness spreads. It certainly fills your tank and allows you to be kinder to others when you start with being kind to yourself. The crazy thing is you'll start to notice others treating you better too. And on the off chance someone *isn't* kind to you, you'll shake it off so much faster because you'll know it's totally about them and *not* you! It will be an anomaly because you can't imagine someone being that way to you on purpose!

5 Practical support

Becoming aware of your thoughts and then learning to choose ones that support you, I won't lie to you, can be exhausting work in the beginning. But know it's just a matter of practice. You don't need to tackle every thought all at once. Just start with the one that gets highlighted to you. And then know that each time you choose to replace that thought with another, you've made progress. Sometimes you'll give in to the old thought, but it won't be long until you're back on the bandwagon of supporting yourself with better choices. You're developing thought muscles. Two steps forward and one step back not only is forward motion, but it's kind of cha-cha! Celebrate the victories one at a time!

Here are ways you can support yourself:

a) **Listen to voices that inspire.** Garbage in, garbage out. Make things as easy for yourself as possible. If watching the news is depressing you, don't. At least for a while. Give yourself a chance to anchor to new ways of thinking. Listen to music that builds you up, listen to podcasts, read authors that support you and encourage you. When you feel good, your mental state is higher and more positive.

b) **Be selective who you share with.** Don't share with the masses. Be a steward of your dreams. Share with those who support them, and shake off those who don't. You don't need their approval or permission, only their support. Surround yourself with people who will cheer you on with encouragement, help you see the bright side, hold your hand when you need it, and make space for tears and triumphs! Surround yourself with people on the journey too.

c) **Write affirmations and practice them.** If it's tough for you to write affirmations, you can order affirmation card decks online as a place to start. I shuffle my decks, set an intention (or say a prayer), and then see which ones pop out of the deck for me as I shuffle. You can shuffle and choose at random. You can pull those on top. It really doesn't matter once you set your intention because you'll get the ones you're supposed to get. So have fun! And then practice them daily to begin shifting your thoughts. Choose new cards when you get the urge to change it up.

d) **Journal.** Not to beat a topic to death, but writing down your thoughts slows you down in a way that you hear yourself. We need to notice our thoughts in order to begin to question them. Are they true? Are they true for everybody? And is there something *more* true that would serve me better? Practice asking questions. You'll be amazed at the answers that come, if not that particular day, over time as you make it a practice to inquire.

One final word…

ACKNOWLEDGE your feelings and have compassion for them, but *CHOOSE your thoughts!*

Section 3

Relationship to Work The Work-Earn-Deserve Paradigm

Chapter 11
Work, Earn, Deserve

As I looked at my relationship to work, this is the equation that emerged: work-earn-deserve. This particular paradigm drives the Western world. See if you can fill in the blanks.

If you want to get ahead, you need to _____.
If you want anything in life, you must be willing to _____ for it.
And if you're not getting ahead, you must not be _____ing _____ *enough*!

If you answered "work hard," you're familiar with this paradigm too! Effort. Hard work. And if you want something badly enough, you must be willing to do *whatever it takes*, or you don't deserve it. And there's the rub. There is an association that successful people sacrifice everything to be successful. And if you're not successful, it's because you're lazy or just not willing to do the hard work, but can I tell you, there are plenty of people working plenty hard enough and somehow just getting by.

I came up against this myself recently as a new realtor while speaking with a more established agent. I was getting ready to list my first house, but my client wanted it to "go live" the day I was leaving for a long-planned trip to attend a friend's retirement celebration. With a crazy real estate market, I really needed to be present to field offers and oversee the open house. What awful timing! Should I cancel my trip or go but plan to work the whole time I was away? I was so tired of making those choices and sacrifices. The experienced agent told me how when she started in real estate, she just decided she would have no life outside of real estate. She would do "*whatever it takes*" to be successful. Well, I had already lived that life with my home staging company while raising four kids. The job came home with me, nights, weekends. My birthday was a nuisance, and holidays, if I were truthful, were inconvenient *and* stressful. I couldn't take time off! How would I get everything done? Yes, I was definitely out of balance and driven. The question was, How did that happen, and *why*? And then how was I to get out of the life I had built? Because the more successful I got, the more I needed to work to sustain it. There were times I was so tired that the thought of continuing on like this for the rest of my life was enough to make me want to die. I didn't see a way out of the endless cycle of hard work. Ever.

And it wasn't just work where I drove myself. I also served in my community in different ways, and while I loved that work, here too, I felt like I could never take time off. Too many people were depending on me. There was always something that needed to be done. *Working hard was a way of life.* I longed for rest, I longed for space, but somehow I couldn't manage to let go long enough to take it.

The desire to just run away and leave it all behind is a pretty common fantasy. We've created lives we don't enjoy living, and we don't know how to extricate ourselves. We don't see a way to change without the drastic step of just anonymously disappearing. Poof, gone, where no one can find us and we can finally have peace and quiet. Most of us suck it up and just keep plodding along wearily.

I've flirted with this fantasy myself. But somehow I knew the problem with running away was that I'd take *myself* with me. I had the firm conviction that unless *I* changed, I would just recreate the same old same old. It might take me a while, but no doubt, I'd end up recreating the life I had just left behind (because I know how to work hard!).

I had just completed a year of examining my compulsion to people-please and was really excited about what I had learned and observed within myself. I had journaled and openly posted my journey on Facebook with the idea of not just changing this dynamic for me but also with the hope that what I had learned would help free others. As I sat facing another year, I began to consider what I would like to leave behind this time as I moved forward into the new year. And I got a strong sense that this time, it wasn't about what I was to leave behind.

Dawn, what is it you want?

And bubbling up from the depths of my being were the words *more joy and ease!*

This truly was what I longed for! I didn't want one more thing to work at, not one more thing. And I ached for it like a woman who had held her breath too long and was drowning. I could see so clearly that the tools I had been using to build my life were the same tools I would need to maintain it. I was working, working, working, hoping one day I could relax and rest. But more success led to *more* hard work. So the question that came to me was if I wanted a life of more joy and ease, could I use joy and ease as the tools to build that life? What would that even look like? I needed to examine the thoughts and beliefs that were preventing me from building a life I actually enjoyed living. Instead of the problem being "out there" where the world wasn't cooperating with me, perhaps the difficulty lay within myself. I suspected I was making life harder than it needed to be.

Let's look at some of the ideas and beliefs around work.

The work-earn-deserve paradigm

This is a merit-based system, and one that is fatally flawed at that! While it seems logical, this equation is part of a scarcity mindset system. There is only so much to go around. You need to work hard and earn. And then you'll only get anything because you've earned it, deserve it, you're *entitled* to it! If you don't get what you want, you're either not working hard enough, or you simply don't deserve it. Those are the only two logical conclusions in this system. And when it doesn't pay out the way we think it should, when others advance who *don't* "deserve" to, we become disillusioned and/or bitter. The system is rigged. Life isn't fair. And that's a hard pill to swallow.

I remember encountering this early in life, running to my mother complaining about one sibling or another and what they had done. My mom would say in a snarky singsong voice, "Well, life isn't always fair, now is it?" How I *hated* that answer! Fix it. Make things right. Make things *fair*, the way my young mind saw fair. I already was being influenced by scarcity and the work-earn-deserve paradigm. Those that deserve, those that don't. I work hard, so I should get; others shouldn't. And with that paradigm or construct, there are serious limitations. My parents were too entrenched in it themselves to be able to help me see something *more*. Their "Life isn't always fair" was more a matter of suck-it-up-and-deal-with-it, rather than let-me-show-you-something-bigger, something better.

The parable of the workers in the field

So I'd like to tell a story, actually a parable, one that Jesus told many years ago. I believe it goes to the heart of the matter. This story challenges how we see reality, and its goal is to set us free from the limits of what we've believed. You've often heard it said, "As above, so below"? Jesus spoke that in another dimension, where he was from, it worked differently. He started the following story with these words, "The kingdom of heaven is like this…"

A landowner had a harvest to bring in, and he needed day laborers. So he gets up early and goes to the marketplace to secure men to work in his vineyard for the day. There he finds many to choose from and hires a large number on the spot. He agrees to pay each of them a day's wage (a denarius) for a day's work, which was then a twelve-hour workday. He then sends them out into his vineyard.

About three hours into the workday, he returns to the marketplace where he sees others just standing around doing nothing. He waves them over with a, "Come on, you can work in my vineyard today too! Help me bring in the harvest, and I will pay you whatever is right." And so they too went, happy to have the work, having families to feed.

Six hours in, then *nine hours* in, twice more the landowner returns to the marketplace. "You want to work? Come with me!

Come work in my vineyard, and I will pay you whatever is right." Off the new hires go to work in the vineyard. Not a full workday perhaps, but it's work, and they have families to feed.

Amazingly, at the eleventh hour, *one hour* before quitting time, the landowner returns once more to the marketplace to gather up whoever is left to work in his field with the promise that he will pay them "whatever is right." And off they go to work the last bit of the workday in the fields.

Now the sun is starting to set, and it's the end of the day. The owner of the vineyard says to his foreman, "Okay, time to stop! Call in the workers and pay them their wages, but start with the last ones hired. Pay them first, and then you can pay the group that I hired at the start of the day, got it?" And so the workers who were hired last lined up, and to their great surprise, they each get paid a *full* day's wage (a denarius). Sweeeet! The original hires are behind them, waiting to get paid, and so you can imagine what they're expecting— *bonuses!* Much to their surprise, they too receive a denarius, a full day's wage. "But that's not fair," they begin to grumble. "After all, we worked a full day out in the hot sun! *We* bore the burden of the work, no fair. These others worked less than us!" And they complained to and against the landowner.

"Friends, why are you complaining? Didn't you agree to work a full day for a full day's wage? Why does it upset you if I am generous?"

Why indeed?

The first group of laborers entered in with the work-earn-deserve paradigm. You work a full day, and you get a full day's wage. Reasonable. Logical. And they had earned and deserved their denarius, and that's what they got. End of story. But this story has a twist because the other workers didn't enter into that same agreement. They simply went to work, and they were only promised that they would receive "whatever is right." There wasn't a dollar amount attached to it. But their agreement allowed for them to receive generously. And what Jesus tells us is that there is a higher, truer reality beyond our 3D, one that is greater, larger, better than the system we could think up. This parable gives us a peek at what's behind the curtain. The work-earn-deserve paradigm is *limiting*.

As I ponder this particular parable, I ask myself, in what ways am I limiting myself because I must work, earn, deserve? Could I possibly be limiting the generous expression of love, not just in money but also in other ways, because I believe I must work hard, earn, and deserve it? If I am being honest, the idea of loosening my grip on this way of thinking is quite unsettling to me, even downright scary. The rigid work-earn-deserve approach at least gives me an illusion of control. And control is about the need for safety. I can control the outcome every time, or so I believe.

Many years ago, as a young singer still in high school, a woman came to a performance in which I was a lead singer in a small group. Afterward, she eagerly greeted me, telling how much she enjoyed the performance and loved my voice. She asked me about my plans, if I was going to college, and yes, indeed I had been accepted as a performance major at the school of my choice. And then she told me she wanted to pay my tuition. What?

And I turned her down.

Yes, I did.

Why couldn't I receive her gift? Why did it make me so uncomfortable that I shut her generosity down? I shake my head at my younger self, the girl who couldn't receive generously and freely, who couldn't receive gifts she hadn't "earned." There are many, many stories like this from my life, each an expression of limitations of belief due to a work-earn-deserve mindset.

I remember my last semester of college scraping by without enough food to eat. My financing had fallen through for my last semester, and so I was working a couple of jobs while student-teaching to complete the requirements to graduate. My boyfriend at the time insisted on taking me to a grocery store where he quite generously bought food for me. I was soooo mad! Why hadn't "God" provided for me so I could buy my own damn groceries? I was so entrenched in a work-earn-deserve mindset that receiving freely from someone else didn't look like love. It looked like lack. I expected to earn my money and provide for *myself*. Wasn't that the way it was supposed to be? To receive generously that which I hadn't earned felt like *failure*. And it was linked to my worth because I didn't deserve it; I hadn't earned it.

It's everywhere in our culture. So much of marketing centers around the message you deserve it, you've earned it, and you're worth it. It's been woven into the very fabric of our cultural message, like our worth is up for grabs. We are hungry to be seen, heard, and cared for. And we're told that material possessions and vacations, as well as other indulgences, will do that for us. And they may...for the moment.

"L'oréal. Because you're worth it."

"You deserve a break today" (old McDonald's jingle).

"Because you deserve the very best" (to sell *toothpaste*, making Crest the top-selling oral hygiene product!).

How often are we told to purchase something because we're worth it? How often are we told to take some time off because we've "earned" it or "deserve" it? I was surprised to have this thought floating into my own mind just the other day when considering an upcoming long weekend away. You deserve it. But I don't want to buy into this way of thinking anymore. This means no longer justifying choices on the basis of earn and deserve. I can simply make the choice because I *want* to, and I *can*. My worth is not up for grabs, and neither is yours. It doesn't need to be proved, earned, voted on, justified, or assigned by anyone or anything outside ourselves. If you want to live a life of generosity and abundance, we're going to need to let go of the things holding us back. And at the top of that list is the work-earn-deserve message. Let's break this down into its components to see where things went amuck.

Chapter 12
Where Did We Go Wrong?

The three components

ork

I'm a big fan of work! As a parent, I've wished for all my kids to discover the joy of working and that work is its own reward. There's something about pushing through obstacles, figuring things out, and achieving a goal that's great for the soul! We learn how to tap into ourselves. We learn how to dig deep within to do things we normally wouldn't do, things that are uncomfortable or that we don't want to do, and in the doing, we discover that somehow it doesn't kill us but makes us stronger. There is a sense of pride that comes with this, and self-esteem is built. *And* we build vital skills like positive self-talk and how to handle and work through difficult emotions like frustration, disappointment, anger. Through work experience, we develop critical thinking skills, time management, and so much more! We build capacity and endurance. These are all beautiful, valuable, rich things! We grow, we learn, we discover, and we become *more*.

Work can be a place to express our creativity, and if the situation doesn't allow for that, we file our ideas away for the future because learning what *not* to do is almost as valuable as learning what *to* do. We learn how to get along with others, when to walk away, and how to communicate better for conflict resolution and achievement of goals. We gain clarity. And we discover we are so much more than we ever imagined. You can see why I'm such a big fan of work!

On the face of things, sounds like work is a great thing. Where does it go wrong? How do things get so out of balance? If the problem isn't in work itself, how about in the earning of it?

Earn

For most of the world, in order for commerce to happen, we have a system of money. We work, we earn money, and then we exchange it for goods, services, and fun. There isn't anything wrong with having this system. It creates a lot of ease throughout the world because we have a common system, money, by which we can trade to get what we need and want. It's just a system, and not a perfect system to be sure. While we can acknowledge the inequities within it, we can also recognize the *system* may not be causing the problem but rather what people bring to it. Abuse can happen within any structure or organization.

But this particular system actually solves a lot of challenges by simplifying the movement of goods and services. We assign value to things (price tag), and people pay with money. Simple. Fast. But it brings other advantages with it as well. This system provides external reward for work done, which is a great starting place when developing a relationship with work. As a parent, until my kids discovered work as its own reward, earning money was a great motivator! Within this system, we can learn things like responsibility—how to manage money and resources, showing up on time, meeting expectations of employers (or possibly parents who are paying you for chores or other jobs). We can become independent and enjoy a sense of freedom, power, and accomplishment. We transition to a larger world and system. While my kids may have rolled their eyes at me for talking to them about character and effort, they got to hear similar principles and teachings in the workplace. Work and earn. And if they didn't work, they lost the opportunity to earn!

Money is not the first place we learn the relationship between working and earning. We encounter this in school for sure where we learn, take tests, earn grades, and progress in our school career. Sports, music, theater, or any place we can accomplish, we work and earn our place on the team or in the system. We persevere when it gets hard because we want the reward. No, it's not perfect, and it doesn't need to be. Even the imperfections carry lessons for us. And we grow creative in navigating these areas until we find our niches and become experts in our own lives and, if not experts, at least seasoned, wise souls.

It's painful, these early lessons, where we want to protect our kids and ourselves from the pain of failure and disappointment, but there's so much richness in being able to navigate those lessons. We are amazingly resilient and incredibly creative.

No, I don't see working and earning as the problem.

Deserve

Here's where things can get sticky, so hang with me, while we challenge some long-held ideas.

We work; we earn. This is great when working for monetary compensation because usually we've made an agreement between parties. Do "X," and get paid "Y." This is transactional and often contractual. So when someone *hasn't* completed the agreed-upon work, they haven't earned payment. We would even say they don't *deserve* payment, at least in the context of the given agreement. But *deserve* is a word of judgment, involving assessment and evaluation; you just can't get around that. Not always bad certainly, but it's helpful to understand its limits. *Deserve* is *subjective* (as much as we want to believe otherwise). And *deserve* is associated with the word *worth*. I find these days I'm watching my use of the word *deserve* when the word *earn* is more fitting.

As someone who has had employees in the running of my home staging business, I can tell you I've been guilty of saying some people were not "worth" the money I was paying them, but I've since dropped that phrase. To be sure, as a business owner, there *is* a cost-to-benefit evaluation to keep a company profitable and to keep the doors open. If someone isn't bringing enough value to my business with their work in relation to cost of having them on my team, it's simply not smart business to keep them. That is a subjective analysis based on available data. An employee may require too much management and oversight when I need more self-direction and responsibility from them. They may be consistently tardy, lack a teamwork mentality, show up unprepared, or break a lot of inventory—all things that raise the cost to me as a business owner. While I may choose to let them go, it's not a pronouncement on their *personal* worth. They just may be unsuited to this job, or they may not be ready for the opportunity of it. That is an important distinction to make, but one we often don't.

This cost-to-benefit evaluation holds true from the employee's side as well. If the cost is too high working a particular job in relation to the benefit we receive, we may say it's "just not worth it." We assess the emotional, physical, and time investment in relation to job satisfaction, financial return, education, and experience. And it's not just the immediate return (many days we would quit otherwise!), but if we're wise, we also keep a bigger picture in mind—our values and our goals. Many of us have put up with short-term discomfort, less-than-desirable work environments, and extra work because we're "getting our foot in the door," "learning the ropes," and/or gaining "valuable work experience," and possibly making important connections with people who may help us along the way.

How many of us have used the phrase, "They don't deserve me," in relation to another person, specifically a boss or even a personal relationship? This is now using *worth* and *deserve* in relation to people. And while placing a value on ourselves is really important and necessary in the getting out of unhealthy and toxic situations, the part that isn't helpful is when we tie it to devaluing or lowering the value of another. "They're just not worth it." In reality, we could simply leave or quit because it's what we want to do and because it's in our best interest. We don't need to justify our decision by elevating our worth and lowering another's. We could simply leave. We could make a decision *for* ourselves instead of *against* another.

Chapter 13

Reward and Punishment

Reward and Punishment

Deserve: de-zerv | verb
Do something or have or show qualities worthy of (reward or punishment)

This requires judgment. Judgments are like lines drawn, instead of in sand, more often etched in stone, inflexible. We believe they're fences we erect, to create order. Mine. Yours. Good. Bad. Saved. Unsaved. Smart. Ignorant. Liberal. Conservative. Right. Wrong. While things *appear* safer and are clearly, cleanly defined in our minds, these judgments also create very real limits. We keep in, but we also shut out. That's one of the limitations of judgments, and we all have them. And while I'm not trying to talk you out of your judgments, I hope to make you more aware of the ways in which you may be limiting yourself. You get to choose. When judgments no longer serve us, we set them down and walk past them into the wide-open meadow beyond the fences we've erected.

It's not always easy to get past judgments or to realize we would benefit from doing so. Most of us are unaware that a huge chunk of our lives are spent reviewing, analyzing, and passing judgment. Someone walks by you at the mall, and you assess how they look without realizing it, making a judgment about who they are and how you stand in relationship to them. At the same mall, a child has thrown himself to the ground, pitching a fit and you think, *I'd never let my child do that* (wait till you have kids of your own), but you may not realize the backstory—a kid who just lost a parent tragically or maybe who is on the autism spectrum, or just simply an overtired mom is merely trying to get something done. We know so little, and yet we feel qualified to judge, or we simply do it reflexively. We're constantly assessing and judging, making pronouncements of who deserves or who doesn't deserve this or that. It's always running in the background. It's the system.

One of my favorite movies these days is *The Unforgivable* with Sandra Bullock, for just this reason. If you want to be challenged, rent it! The story opens with a woman being released from prison after serving out her sentence for killing a police officer—the unforgivable crime. Little by little bit, you get new information, and it's like the screenwriter asks, "What do you think *now*?" with each new revelation. "How about *now?*" I love how this movie challenges our tendency to judge and assign worth on limited information.

I find I'm more careful with my language these days. Earning is one thing. Worth—I'm now stepping into an arena I shouldn't with another. People are worth loving. People are worth respecting. And when they make poor choices, those things are not withdrawn, even when boundaries need to be set. In fact, Matt Kahn points out in his "All for Love" platform that when people make poor choices, they need *more* love, not less. But in the end, I get to choose who *I* am. I used to tell my kids, "Every day, you choose who you will be." Others need not dictate who we are and how we behave. It is not on the basis of deserve.

Many of us get this deserve thing confused at an early age. When parents or people on whom we depend withdraw love or approval because we haven't performed or met expectations or needs, we associate those things with our worth. I grew up in a house that not only had a lot of yelling, with the toxic words, "You should be ashamed of yourself," but also withdrew love by giving the silent treatment, often after being yelled at. I remember vividly my father telling me after I ran away from home that I was breaking up the family, causing problems they didn't otherwise have. I was in so much pain I didn't know where to go or how to cope, but what was expressed was how I was destroying our family. And then came the silent treatment of disapproval. Later, when I went away to college and decided to concentrate on my studies instead of returning home every weekend, my father traveled the distance to tell me, "Don't come home. We don't want you." The longest silent treatment I received was nearly 2 1/2 years where my father would barely speak to me. When I called home, he would simply hand the phone over to my mother. These were pretty painful times where I worked desperately to earn my father's love and approval. I remember one phone conversation where my father asked in frustration what I wanted from him. My reply was simple. "I just need you to tell me you love me." "I will not," he replied. I got off the phone and threw up. Neither one of us benefitted from this dynamic. I never could do enough to earn and keep it. As far as he was concerned, he withheld his love because I didn't deserve it. So why do we do this to each other? Because we have carried the work-earn-deserve paradigm into all areas of our lives.

And for many of us, it's killing us.

Let's talk about some of the ways work-earn-deserve shows up.

Chapter 14
The Ways Work-Earn-Deserve Show Up

These are by no means the only ways this paradigm shows up in our lives, but they are some of the most common. Let's dive in.

1 Fear of missing out

I was recently talking with a friend who was offered the job of a lifetime. I mean, it was really big! But it was going to be a long, slow process to get through all the red tape and bureaucracy involved in getting vetted and all the pieces falling into place. Still, it was pretty exciting! In the meantime, he landed an incredible opportunity under someone he really respected and trusted. For the first time in perhaps his life, he wasn't grinding it out and had room to breathe with great money and time to enjoy it. It was just what he was asking for at this season in his life! With some additional family responsibilities on his plate that required more of his time, this new position allowed him to be there for his family member, a core value, and *still* have time for himself. But lo and behold, within a short time of settling into the new position, you guessed it, the other job materialized—the once-in-a-lifetime sort of opportunity. And so he called me to process.

What he'd been told was, "Steven, we've created this position *just for you.* We really want you on our team heading this thing up. And I gotta tell you, if you turn it down, this sort of thing only comes *once in a lifetime.* You won't get another chance like this. (No pressure!) And by the way, this is probably only for one year because generally people burn out after a year."

So on the one hand, you have a great position which allows time to care for your family, time to breathe after a lot of run, run, run, perform, perform, perform...*and* time to care for yourself, with great money and great possibilities. Behind door number 2 is the "once in a lifetime" opportunity, created *just for you* (oh, and if you're a high-performing people-pleaser, this is quite the hook!). *And* they just told you, while telling you no problem, you can still take time to care for your family situation in this high-paced, high-profile job where you'll be traveling all the time, people typically burn out after a year because the job is intense. But you know, it's only for a year; surely you can crank it out for another year, right? After all, it's a *once-in-a-lifetime, you'll-never-have-this-opportunity-again* sort of thing.

I totally get it. I listened, I mirrored back key phrases to my friend, but the truth of the matter, I told him he couldn't get it wrong. Where he was at was bringing in new joy and ease in his life, true, but door number 2 *was* an incredible opportunity. And door number 1 would still be open to him after his year spent behind door number 2. Knowing my friend, if he walked through that door number 2, he would totally knock their socks off! Everything he does, he does well. But at what cost to himself? And what did he *want*? And so we finished our conversation, and I trusted he would make the best decision for himself at this time. And he decided to stay where he was at. What a brave choice!

What was interesting was the hook. *Once in a lifetime.* Does anyone see the underlying scarcity of this phrase? Do you feel the *fear* behind it? If I get this wrong, I will miss out. I will not get the "reward," and in fact, I will be punished for not pushing through to take advantage of this incredible thing. I must push through, work hard, or miss out. That's it, no other opportunities. You had your shot! (You don't deserve another.)

I watch this scenario play out again and again around me and feel the pull of it in my own life. I have another friend who's always picking up an extra job here and there, ignoring the aches and pains of a body in protest, just to earn that little bit extra that additional contract work affords. It won't be there for her if she doesn't. Or that's the paradigm. I struggle with this too. I remember being a single parent (the first time around) working three jobs with kids with special medical challenges. The hours I put in to make ends meet, sometimes to two or three in the morning! And I remember the day I heard the voice inside that said, "Dawn, how would you like to give up one of these jobs and still get by?" What? That's just nuts, or was it? And so I quit one of the jobs which was bringing in another $800/month (a fortune at the time to me), and somehow the ends still met at the end of each month. I don't rightly know how.

I'm not saying go out and quit your job (or one of them), but I *am* asking you to question your paradigm and the beliefs you have around work-earn-deserve. I'm learning to be suspicious when fear is driving me. When fear shows up, instead of running headlong *into* something or *away* from something else, I stop to pause and take a closer look. Am I making a decision because I'm afraid of missing out? Do I really need to drive myself this hard?

2 Fear of stepping off the prescribed path

"Danger, Will Robinson, danger!" Don't you know there's a prescribed path, the RIGHT way to live your life, have relationships, raise kids, be healthy (the ideal weight and body type), etc., and when you don't follow it, disasters happen? "You've no one but yourself to blame," says the voice inside our heads and often the refrain around us. We are told every day how we *should* be living life (and it changes with every generation, believe me). If you're following the prescribed path, it's *easy*, they tell you! It's only hard if you *don't* do it the right way. In case you're not clear on it, someone will happily voice their opinion on what you should be doing. Gosh, it's not easy being different. And in some way or another, we all are. We can hide it, cover it up, deny it, and then double down and follow the rules. But for many of us, it's really killing us.

Maybe we're listening to the wrong voices. There's a body of voices who have been really loud and have been controlling the narrative for the rest of us. And what they are doing works for *them.* Fantastic! But what if it's not working for *me*? What if I'm not like *them*? The narrative then is that I will not have a good life, *and it will be my fault!*

When I started my home staging company, I was told by an expert in personality profiling that I wasn't wired to be a successful businesswoman. I didn't have the right personality type to do it well. My business would flounder and most likely fail. No offense, but I should find a different career path, I was told. As a creative, I needed to let someone else lead; creatives are too flighty, too disorganized. They don't have staying power. Well, that didn't sit right with me, thankfully, even though I had tons of respect for the person telling me this. I had vision and passion. And yet I still struggled with the idea that I wasn't "wired" right. Maybe I was too sensitive, my morals and ethics too restricting, meaning I didn't have what it takes to get ahead in business, as some said. Didn't you have to be tough to run a business? I was soft and tenderhearted. But I was tough in ways that they and I didn't yet understand. So yes, I started my home staging business, and I was really, really good at it. And I got better as I embraced the many fabulous lessons I needed to become successful. And with each lesson learned, a new level of growth happened, in myself and in my business. But I built my company in the way that was congruent to me and my core values. And you guessed it, creativity and relationships were at the center of my business model. My sensitivity and creativity were my superpowers! Who knew? It's *hard* to challenge the current messaging! And it takes a lot of courage!

If the prescribed path doesn't fit, it's not the right one for you! It's okay to spend a little time on the path. You learn some great things, but when it starts to destroy you inside, it's probably time to carve out a different path. Just because it's a new path doesn't mean disaster waits around the corner. Challenges await you for sure. After all, you may be paving the new road someone else will follow later. It takes work, and there will be nights you doubt yourself. The voices of the prescribed path are strongest in the dark.

It took an incredible amount of courage to leave my first marriage, and it was messy! I was the first of my friends to get divorced, and I was the first in my particular faith community. Oh, and didn't we all learn on one another! I endured the judgments and pronouncements of many around me, how I wasn't trying hard enough. Obviously, I wasn't committed enough to my marriage. I wasn't *godly* enough (well, the latter may have been true!). We all had a paradigm, myself included, that if one worked hard enough, you could make anything work. I just needed to suck it up and keep going. I needed to have *faith*. And I tried; I really did. I tried it all, using every tool I had at the time, but it was destroying me, and it was destroying my health, which ultimately meant that I was "weak," according to the narrative. And so I tried some more. I actually believed at one point that I could have a successful marriage as long as *one* of us in the marriage was willing. And when I decided to leave, it broke me. I felt betrayed. I had followed the prescribed path after all and *failed*. I thought my life was over; I wanted to die. So much inside that I had pushed down came up to the surface in the breaking, and it wasn't pretty. But in daring to step out from the prescribed path, I found a new and better life for myself. I found a new and better me. And though it was messy and seemingly disastrous, there was this fabulous life waiting on the other side when I chose to follow the path of my heart and the voice inside me versus the ones around me.

Many of the voices around you mean well. By all means, listen to those older and wiser than yourself. You'd be foolish not to, but if their message seems dissonant with your own inner voice, take some time to process and evaluate. Listen to the voice within, your inner knowing. Remember, others are not experts on *your* life. Only you are.

3 Fear of punishment

While this overlaps with the last one, fear of punishment bears looking at on its own. I joke I'm not even Catholic, but I suffer from Catholic guilt! It really is deeply embedded in our society—the fear of punishment. I remember the narrative when AIDS appeared on the scene. It was God's punishment for people stepping outside the lines. We immediately go there, most of us, instead of the place of compassion. Disaster and hardship are evidence of punishment. Why is that?

Fear of punishment is the place I go in the middle of the night. I didn't do enough, I didn't get enough right, and now I'm afraid I will be punished, and the good I had hoped for will be withheld from me. I will not be *blessed*. The work-earn-deserve paradigm at its classic! There's a prevalent idea among God-*fearing* people that we've never done enough. God wants to bless us, but he's just shaking his head when he looks at us and sighing with disappointment. I suspect we've made a God in the image of our own limitations and then defend our inability to love ourselves and others. The idea that God is just waiting to zap us when we step out of line is a means that religious communities, society, and even our parents have used to keep us on the aforementioned prescribed path. Fear of punishment is just an overall dread that can reside within us unexamined. We don't have to do anything *wrong,* that we know of. We just believe we haven't done *enough* to deserve good things. There's always something left undone. Wow, there's just something wrong with that perspective, don't you think? And what a miserable way to live.

Dread is just another word for this fear. It's usually more generalized, not really attached to one thing per se. It rarely tells you the full truth, and it will keep you running like a chicken with its head cut off...or at the least living the prescribed path without questioning it. Your inner knowing will be more reliable than the nonspecific, generalized voice of fear. Have a listen for sure, meet it with the tools of curiosity and compassion, but tune in deeper.

4 Fear of others

If you found yourself in the section on people-pleasing, then you already know what I mean here! But the truth of it is this. No matter who you are, people and their opinions matter at some level. You may care about a small group, you may care about a large group, but we all need a place to belong. We're social creatures who need a tribe, a community, a place of belonging, and without it, we waste away. From human development research, we know that babies who have all their physical needs met but are not held die. Healthy brain development is tied to the interactions between infants and their caregivers. And scientists know the best predictor of health (besides smoking) is the quality of our relationships with others. In short, connection and contact with others is a basic biological need, and when met, our immune systems are stronger, our heart and respiratory rates are regulated, and we have greater stress resilience. It has been shown that social isolation and loneliness can increase a person's odds of an early death by 25–30%![2]

Throughout history, being put out of our community meant almost certain death because of our dependence on others for survival. Even today, to be ostracized and put out of our communities can be painful and frightening beyond words...mentally, emotionally, and physically. We see these effects with the rise of cyberbullying. To be ostracized and/or isolated can be deadly. So much for the old adage, "Sticks and stones may break my bones, but words will never hurt me"!

In a world that screams for tolerance, we really mean compliance. Be like us, think like us, live like us, and then you can live among us. So the fear of others can be a really strong pull. The most painful part of the breakup of my first marriage was the loss of community. Longtime friends who didn't approve of my choices no longer spoke to me and even talked behind my back. Letters and phone calls went out to different people without my knowledge, warning them against me and against talking to me. Yes, stepping outside the lines can be dangerous. But the slower death is staying among a group of people from whom you need to hide your true thoughts, beliefs, and feelings, or ones with whom you must sacrifice yourself to be accepted.

As parents, we want our kids to be happy, but so often we want them to be happy *our way*. We want our friends to follow our advice and do things our way because it affirms us in *our* life choices. And

---

[2] *Burnout: The Secret to Unlocking the Stress Cycle* by Emily Nagoski, PhD, and Amelia Nagoski, DMA.

it's just more comfortable for us when people are like us. But how boring the world would be without diversity and the challenges that comes from it! In truth, I can affirm others' life choices while I choose my own. And others can do the same for me.

Those who truly are your friends will allow you to grow and change. Those who don't aren't your people. They may have been at one time, but maybe the next leg of the journey, you'll need different traveling companions, a new tribe. So if you find yourself with the decision of choosing *yourself* or choosing the people in your life, consider the long view. You're the one you're going to go through life with. Invest well in yourself, and trust there are others who will want to be in your circle.

5 Fear: If it's easy, I must be cheating

(And that makes me bad, right?) I don't deserve it. I haven't suffered enough. Oh, the brainwashing of work-earn-deserve! And we look around at others who are working so hard, complaining, grinding it out, and if it's too easy for us, we think we're doing something wrong. And we may even feel guilty about if we're not suffering or working hard enough.

For a period of time when my three oldest children were little, I did direct sales with a company I loved. Their motto, "Products in Harmony with Nature and Good Health," was revolutionary at the time when green products were hard to come by and health was a matter of being thin or simply a result of your genes, i.e., the luck of the draw. I was so excited by the idea that I could build my health intentionally as well as live harmoniously with the earth. Loving the products and seeking a way to bring in money while being a stay-at-home mom, this opportunity was for me! I got to do what I love—help others, make a difference in the world, AND contribute to our family's financial stability. Score! And I was building my own personal health to boot! I loved what I was doing and was quite good at it. Before long, I had earned a brand-new car, a minivan, quite exciting in its day, and something that would benefit our growing family. When it arrived fresh off the lot, I was sooooo embarrassed and self-conscious! I remember the first time I drove it to my church, and someone made the sarcastic comment, "Boy, must be nice." The judgment I received from people who believed I had come by it easily without enough effort mirrored my own thoughts and fears. I hadn't worked hard enough to deserve a car like that. And I felt guilty.

That's one way the work-earn-deserve paradigm shows up. If you don't follow the rules of hard work (and who gets to measure that, really?), you feel *guilty*, and the world will tell you you should because you've somehow cheated the system. And so if you're not aware of it, you'll find a way to make your life harder...because you know you're not allowed to have it easy. No fair, everyone else will say. No fair, your own self will tell you, and then you'll sabotage. You'll take the job that's harder with people who are more difficult to work with. You'll choose the job where you're putting in more hours because that's what it looks like to be a good, responsible person. You'll stay with a person who is really tough to live with because, after all, that's what commitment looks like. And we'll stay past the point where we should. Life's supposed to be hard, and if it's not, you must be taking shortcuts somewhere. Good people don't cheat. Good people don't take shortcuts. Good people have it *hard*.

In challenging that belief, what kind of life opens up for us? Well, when I get my work done early and my life has space, I have more to contribute to others—time, energy, resources, JOY. I like that aspect. I can invest in growing and learning with my extra time (I love free time!). And because I believe the world is better served by my joy than my suffering, I can just rest, relax, and have fun! That too serves the world. So let life be easy where you can and hard where it must. When we challenge the work-earn-deserve paradigm, we can look for the ways where life doesn't need to be hard!

6 Hardship bias

The Hard Thing = The Right Thing

I had a decision to make the other day, and all of a sudden, I realized I carried this equation in my head: if it's hard to do, it must be the right thing to do. Ugh, and I almost fell for it again! It's one of the ways I've made my life harder than it needed to be. I've had a difficulty bias…not against it but *for* it! Well, now that I see it, it does seem a bit silly really. But it rears its head still now and again, and when it does, I can weigh in with my inner knowing and give myself permission to make the choice I *want* to make. Often it's the easier one for me. Everything does NOT have to be hard!

Realizations that are changing my life are the following:

- Just because I *can* doesn't mean I *should*. (This will free up a lot of time and energy!)
- Hard does not necessarily mean *better*. It just means *hard*. (That'll make you think twice!)

7 Suffering gives you street cred

The fear here is people won't respect you if you don't suffer enough ('cause you know, you cheated the system!). They won't listen to you because you haven't earned your place among them. What could you possibly know and contribute?

There will always be someone who tells you your voice doesn't count, and why. I'll let you in on a little secret. It doesn't matter how much you suffer or don't; unless someone is ready to listen, they won't hear you. And if people are measuring meaning and importance by suffering and hard work, there will always be someone willing to suffer more and work harder or those who feel like their suffering matters more than yours. They will tell you yours doesn't count and then tell you why. You haven't had it as hard as they have, let me tell you.

Those who have truly learned life lessons in their suffering tell their story differently. They typically don't rehearse them over and over again, telling you how hard they've had it. It is not a contest or a point of comparison. In fact, those who have deepened through life's challenges hold room for the stories of others, often only sharing their own details when helpful. They listen with greater compassion and wisdom than those who have not learned but have only experienced. They're more likely to get in the boat you're rowing, keep you company, maybe wipe your brow, and cheer you on than to criticize your technique.

By the way, the reverse is true too. For some, you will have suffered too much, and so they will distance themselves, wondering what's wrong with you. It's the judgment thing. We almost can't help ourselves unless we intentionally live with mindfulness. It's possible! So live your life! And know you will draw the people and opportunities that are a match to you. Let go of your own judgment with regard to hard work and suffering so you don't create it unnecessarily in your life.

8 I should be able to do more.

Distorted expectations and comparisons.

This is a big one for me! One of the unfortunate things of social media is we are able to view others at their best and highest moments. And you know, we never measure up. While we see *their* brightest and best, we're home cleaning toilets, wiping runny noses, cutting the grass, and changing air filters (man, I'm way overdue with those!), or maybe cleaning up from a sick dog. When their selfie at the gym pops up on our feed, we catalog another day we skipped our workout because our kid forgot their school lunch, and we had to run it over, never mind that we made it to the gym the last three days in a row! There is this constant, generalized guilt saying that we're just somehow missing the mark. Other people are out there doing more than you are, and they're *killing* it!

Compare and despair.

You should be able to do it all and more, and then with a smile on your face! Work hard, but make it look easy. And so we're questioning *ourselves* rather than the system.

This judgment is born from measuring things undone rather than those done. It comes from comparing others' public image to how we feel inside and the realness of our own lives. And sometimes it comes from the mistaken belief that we should be able to change that which is not ours to change. It is the voice of guilt and shame. And it's meant to keep you in line.

This voice comes with a plague of shoulds and shouldn'ts. Why are you so tired (hear the underlying judgment you "shouldn't" be)? This is the voice of the external world rather than the voice within. The only cure is to connect with ourselves and listen to our inner voice, to let *that* voice grow stronger. And *then* we challenge the system, not by tearing it down (though some of you may have this calling) but by no longer feeding it. If the voice within is my best guide, I am faced daily with the choice of being true to myself or bowing to the pressure of external voices, what "they" say I should do. It's our choice to not bow to the voice of guilt and shame.

When I worked in corporate America, I remember how torn I was going home with work still in my inbox. I always felt the pressure of staying late to get it all done. It seems there is *always* work to be done, another mountain to climb. That was the same pressure I've carried into parenting, keeping house, meeting the needs of others, and running my own business. These days, I'm leaning in on the side of that still small voice. Sometimes it tells me taking a nap is more important than writing. Sometimes it says, "You're done for the day," even when I didn't accomplish all I had planned. It says, "Trust the process," and then encourages me to leave stuff undone for another day in order to live and enjoy life, in order to care for myself. I should be able to do more? Hmmmm, *should* I? And do I *want* to? If there's a contest out there for who's doing the most, I want out. You win. I'm not playing that game anymore. I'm following my joy.

9 Who do you think you are?

Why should things be any easier for *you*?

Imagine something different for yourself, and someone will tell you why it won't work, and then they'll look at you like you're crazy. And if you don't listen, they'll resort to shaming you. If they can't get you with shoulds and shouldn'ts, they'll get you with, "Who do you think you are?"

"Who do you think you are?" the governing group of men at my church challenged me as a young woman when I asked for their support. I planned to quit my job teaching to take a year off to travel with a musical whose theme was God's love. (You would think they would be pro this idea!) Would they back me?

"Who do you think you are?" challenged my daughter's pre-school teacher when I took her off processed sugar to help her with some emotional swings. "You're an abusive mom, denying your kids sugar," said one. "Your kids will be ostracized," said another. (By the way, they were just fine, and turns out, I was just ahead of my time.)

"Who do you think you are?" challenged my dad when I chose something different from family beliefs and expectations for my life. Who are you to think life can be different for *you*? Do you think you're *better* than us? Not better, no, but different perhaps. And for every time I stood up to someone else's, "Who do you think you are?" there were hundreds of internal ones that kept me small and made me doubt myself.

Who do you think you are to write a book (that someone will read)?

Who are you to think you'll be successful?

Who are you to build a life of joy and ease?

Who are you to be *happy*?

The who-do-you-think-you-ares will talk you out of your dreams, keep you small and "safe," and have you regularly biting your tongue, burying the voice within.

Years ago, I attended a community meeting where everyone was agreed on a course of action, and I strongly disagreed. Who was I to speak up? Obviously, majority is always right. And yet I realized I needed to speak up because I represented a minority position. And what I did I find? When I spoke up, there were others who had been holding their tongues too. Who-do-you-think-you-are will tell you to sit down and shut up and don't rock the boat in word or deed. It will make you question *yourself*.

The only way to deal with who-do-you-think-you-are is not to get in an argument with it. Just be yourself. *Practice* being yourself with courage (one of our three Cs). Experiment. May the voice within of your truest self grow stronger with each day. Speak up. Pursue the dream, and if you're not ready to take action, journal, write down your ideas and hopes and dreams. Fan those flames, and then listen within for the right time and the right opportunities. Don't be afraid to prepare for them because they're coming.

Who do you think you are? You're YOU. And I'm so glad! Can I just take a moment to say a thank-you to each of you who steps out with such courage? I'm in awe of you.

Chapter 15
Shifting from a Work-Earn-Deserve Mindset

Practical help

We feel the pressure of this system pressing from outside ourselves, and certainly the internal pressure of it. We've named some of the ways this shows up in our lives. But how do we begin to shift away from seeing the world through this lens? Here are some tools I've found along the way.

1 Drop the word *deserve* from your vocabulary.

At least just for now. It will force you to examine your thinking every time you would've used the word, kinda like tying one arm behind your back makes you notice everything you do in a day. You'll suddenly have thoughts like, *Is this really what I want to say? Is this what I mean? Is there a better word?* And consider this. Are you justifying your choices with its use? Do you need to justify them, and *why?*

"I deserve that piece of chocolate cake." (We may not say it aloud, but we think it!)

Just eat the piece of cake if you want it. Or don't. But it's far simpler to do that than complicating the choice by justification and/or guilt. And then if you want to work out before or afterward because your health and trim figure are important to you, do that too! If we

119

eat the cake and we don't "deserve" it, we then beat ourselves up, which doesn't help the situation. If you want to motivate yourself to go to the gym, try this. "I choose self-care because I love myself, and it is in alignment with my highest good." It's much simpler if we own our decisions rather than give our power away by defending or justifying them…to ourselves or others. It's *cleaner.* Can you feel that?

The difficulty with justifying choices with "deserve" is we also justify choices that *aren't* good for us. Another drink. Another hour of TV binging (my vice of choice). I've had a hard day, so I "deserve" to…fill in the blank. Those things, in my experience, lead to feeling regret afterward. If I drop "deserve," I now get to ask better questions of myself. "What do I need that would support me right now?" It's not that a drink or a night of TV-binging is necessarily bad, but inside this system of deserve, we'll live more in reaction than intention, justification instead of aligned choices.

Those of us who have the tendency to overwork, taking the word *deserve* out of our vocabulary helps us live more kindly with ourselves. Without it, we must reconnect to *ourselves,* tuning into our bodies and emotions for inner guidance, to tell us when we need to take breaks or step away for a moment or go to bed early and get a fresh start tomorrow. It's a different way to live. I'm much more likely to take a nap now, and my body thanks me as well as those around me! I get to be a much nicer version of myself after a nap! How beautiful is that? Direct, intentional, and aligned. Dropping the word *deserve* will do a lot to set us free from the outer messages of the world's current system of work-earn-deserve.

And without the word *deserve* and the driving idea behind it, how would our relationships with others change? They too become cleaner. I don't have to "deserve" my friends, and they don't have to "deserve" me (phew!). We choose to love and be in relationship with one another, and they do the same. Choice. When we must move on or part ways, when we must set boundaries to be able to love ourselves and love the best version of another, we make the decision cleanly and process the emotions we have around it. And contrary to what you'd expect, dropping the word *deserve* means you'll set *better* boundaries. Only weak boundaries demand the word *deserve.*

And what about the person who gets something they *don't* deserve, who didn't *earn* it? Let it go. If goodness comes into the lives of people we don't believe have earned or deserve it, well, then letting that judgment go also releases us from the same measure. I can live a life where goodness flows without me having to work to deserve it!

Yes, let's drop *deserve* from our vocabulary. This will help you see yourself and the world in a whole different light and have you noticing all the ways this belief system of work-earn-deserve has crept in to take over, with all its limitations.

This leads me to the next tool.

2 The four guiding questions

These four questions are MAGIC, freeing us from the shoulds and ought-tos that have us scrambling to earn and deserve. They will help us stay on track to live a life of joy and ease.

1. Is this in alignment with my CORE VALUES?

What are core values? These are the nonnegotiable in our lives, the things we consider to be the most important, what we *value*. And when we are clear on them, they become the plumb line by which we measure our days. Are we on track? Are we off track? When making decisions, we check first whether it is in alignment with our core values. The expression of these may change through the years, but the core values themselves do not. They are our priorities. And if we don't discover and name them, others will do it for us! The world is quite happy to tell us what our priorities should be! And make no mistake, when others name your priorities, it is usually in service to themselves and not you.

As a business owner, one of my core values was excellence. I wanted to exceed the expectations of my clients, outperform my competitors, and utilize one of my other core values—creativity—in getting the jobs done in a way that wowed customers and made us unique. I didn't want to create cookie-cutter experiences and "turn 'em out" fast. I wasn't interested in being the cheapest; I wanted to be the *best*! I wanted to set the standard in my industry of what great staging was. So when we were losing bids to companies who would do it cheaper, I had a decision to make. Do a lower-quality job to cut costs and end up hating what I was doing, or find a way to build my business and my brand on *value* and our commitment to excellence. When I got clear, my marketing changed, who I hired changed, and my clients changed. I drew the clients and people who were in alignment with this particular core value. And I ended up with a company and work that excited me.

Core values are discovered as we live our lives, and we may wrongly assume everyone holds the same ones we do! I remember the first sit-down to name and put in writing the core values of my company. I had never done anything like this before despite being in business over a decade. My assistant at the time was writing words like *fun*, *play*, and *adventure*, while I was writing down words like *excellence*, *creativity*, *problem-solving*, and *strong work ethic*. Through that exercise, it became clear we were not wanting to work at the same company! (She left; I didn't, ha ha ha). It's not about right or wrong. It is about *prioritization*. I've no doubt my former assistant found or created a company that echoed her core values (who knows, she may be a cruise director today)!

In my personal life, core values have me turning off my phone when I pick my daughter up from school these days, taking more time off to give her the extra time, attention, and support she needs after a tough loss this year. I'm clear about what's important to me, and then I'm making decisions of how to walk that out through the different seasons of life. Brené Brown talks about prioritizing courage over comfort. And she certainly lives a life that exemplifies that—an introvert who speaks openly with incredible transparency to thousands of people, speaking about tough subjects. Prioritization. Alignment.

Reviewing core values gave me clarity to leave a marriage that, while I loved my husband, was destroying my health. It was eye-opening to talk frankly and realize we had no shared core values on which to build. Not one. And because I value my well-being and my health, I released myself, and I released him.

Putting our core values into words will be one of the greatest exercises to keep work-earn-deserve from stealing your time, energy, and attention from what's important to YOU. Is this in alignment with my core values? If the answer is no, why would you say yes to it?

2. Is this the right time for this particular opportunity/person? Do I have the time and inner resources to take this on? (Remember the fear of missing out!)

I'm an idea person. I get excited by opportunities and possibilities, but after checking to see if something is in alignment with my core values, I next check with myself to see if it's the right time to take something new on. I'll be honest, it involves a little bit of trial and error figuring out the best balance point for our lives, and that balance point changes over different seasons of life. I've often underestimated the time something would take and overestimated my resources. If you're like me (human), at some point, you're going to take on too much, and it will be a great learning experience! Those of us coming out of a work-earn-deserve paradigm have a tendency to take on too much, so asking if this is the right time is a wise thing to consider. Sometimes we need to pass on a good thing because it's simply not the right time, trusting that more good things are in our future. The one appearing today may be a foreshadowing of that something wonderful ahead of us. And so we let these pass by, trusting that the things that are supposed to be in our lives will be.

I remember looking for what seemed a very long time for the right property that would allow me to build a warehouse for my business. I looked and looked and went through the disappointment of things not working out for one reason or another. And each one I had to turn down because the location wasn't quite right or the price was too high, I would repeat to myself, if I think this one's great, the one that's coming must be even better! This is what it looks like to hold hope while honoring ourselves by waiting for the right time. Not the perfect time, but the right time.

3. Is there JOY here?

Ask your heart and not your head. How do you feel when you think about this? What is the *overriding* emotion? How does it feel in your body when you think about this decision? This is really key. If you feel tense or heavy or even tired, you may not be in alignment with the decision you're making. Don't blow past that without a closer look. If you feel excited and light, buoyed up, or energized, there's joy there. And feel free to follow joy! You'll figure out the how-tos. You'll find solutions for any challenges. Joy is really creative when it wants something!

So "let your YES be YES and your NO be NO." While we think this is simply an admonishment to be a person of our word, as I was always taught, I think if we take a closer look, there's deeper wisdom here. What does it mean to let your "yes be yes and your no be no?" Alignment. How often do we say yes to things that we really want to say no to? And how often are we saying no to things we really want to say yes to? When we allow ourselves to listen to our hearts and our bodies, we have access to our inner knowing, our inner wisdom. And when we say yes or no from *this* place, we have what one of my friends calls the full-body YES or the full-body NO. Don't worry if you don't know what that feels like yet. You've trained yourself to ignore these signals as unimportant in the world of duty and work-hard, do-what-you're-supposed-to. You'll start to tune in again with some practice. This is what we talked about in section 2. If you don't catch it before you've made a decision you regret, you'll catch it with your twenty-twenty hindsight. That's actually fabulous! Stopping to look for the moment you blew past an inner objection or body clue is super valuable! It won't be long till you begin catching it before you say that unwanted yes or no! You'll become aware of how your body feels and how your heart feels. And then you practice making decisions from that place, building a *new* habit for yourself. This is part of *higher*-level adulting—staying in alignment. Make a commitment to love yourself enough to stay in alignment. And have compassion as you learn and practice.

It's interesting to watch my fourteen-year-old go through this already. She's experiencing the split between the head and the rest of herself (heart and body), which leaves her driving herself too hard with her school assignments. She feels such pressure and stress! I know this separation too, when I don't heed all parts of myself, and it generally leads to a meltdown or a flare of temper. "My head tells me to keep going, but my heart and body say it's time for a break," she told me this morning after processing a really stressful night of catching up on assignments from when she was out sick. And so we practice. It's not that we never need to dig deep to find resources to complete tasks or care for the people around us, but we always seek alignment with ourselves. We seek to do these things with the wisdom of our whole selves. And when we go forth in our alignment, we are open to find and create solutions that work. You'll continue to learn and hone these skills over a lifetime!

4. Is this the highest and best use of my time and resources right now?

This is a life-changing question! Sometimes we jump in to do something that is best delegated. Those are the times we'd be better off allowing someone else to step forward to volunteer. If we are to stay in alignment with our core values, that means saying no to some things that come our way. It's not because you're too good to serve or do small tasks, but if your highest and best is called elsewhere, not asking this question means you're going to get sidetracked and tricked by shoulds and ought-tos.

When training new head stagers whose tasks were to come up with the design for each project, run the crew on-site and decide any changes that needed to be made to hold the integrity of the design; it was a question that I constantly posed to my head stagers. When they'd be tempted to run out to the truck to get a supply, to personally see to the missing light bulb in a lamp, or to run to take care of each small task they saw needing to be done, I'd stop them with, "Wait. Is this your highest and best use right now?" Most of the time, it wasn't. We had assistants for that work. So they needed to learn to delegate the tasks that others could do in order to free them up for their highest and best use, making sure the design was executed with excellence. When other people can put in a missing light bulb and there's only one person in charge of making decisions such as do we need additional art for camera angles, staying in their highest and best use *serves everyone*. This then becomes a very powerful, clarifying question! In the same way, there's only one you. What is *your* highest and best use? I wish someone had taught me this principle as a parent. I would have had my oldest children contribute way more to save my sanity and energy, keeping me in my highest and best use as their mom! Too often I was the cleanup committee picking up all the other tasks that didn't get done or no one wanted to do. I would have had way more space and time to be my best self as a parent with a lot more joy and ease!

A Word of Encouragement

Keep in mind, you really can't get it wrong. We practice, we learn, we grow, and we get better. You may take another lap around the learning track, but then it's just another opportunity to practice compassion for yourself and others. It takes a while! That's why we practice. And *do* take time to look closely when fear shows up so you don't make the same decisions you've always made and then get surprised at the same result. That would be crazy, right?

Chapter 16
Joy in the Journey

Higher up and Deeper In

How can we have more joy and ease in our lives? By identifying some of the ways we are blocking its flow with our belief systems, structures, and triggers. That's what I hope this book has done for you, causing you to look at yourself and your life in a different way, from a different perspective. It's wonderful to have knowledge; it's another to digest it until it becomes a part of us so that it manifests in the way we live and the way we relate to others. We go higher up and deeper in, to paraphrase C. S. Lewis. And honestly, that takes a while—a lifetime in fact. Perhaps many lifetimes. It's never reaching a finish line where we can say, "There! I've got it down now." It's simply that we become more practiced. Perfecting, ever perfecting, while never seeking perfection.

That's a tough line to keep at first.

When we measure our days in accomplishing things and crossing them off a checklist, we often look for the finish line. That's where we're used to finding our value, an old cultural habit.

"There, I'm over people-pleasing."

I haven't reached that point myself yet. I continue to discover the places where I can go higher up and deeper in.

Here, now I've achieved perfect health and balance in listening to the wisdom of my body."

Instead, I continue to learn the language of my body.

"Done! I have no more unchallenged thoughts. I have a perfectly disciplined mind. There always seems to be new ground to take here when I experience new things and their accompanying challenges.

If your goals are to cross some imaginary finish line, you're going to have serious trouble building a life of joy and ease. The line of growth always moves as we grow and expand, along with our capacity to hold more of life. There is no finish line of forever perfection. So we must learn a new way to measure our days and have joy in the journey.

Here are some suggestions.

1 Build a culture of celebration

Begin by building your own counterculture. *Celebrate yourself,* each small win. Acknowledge new thoughts and the aha moments, even when you miss an opportunity to follow through. We're going to *actively look* for things to celebrate. You see, it's not about perfection but *progress*. It's about respecting and embracing the journey as it is, each step. New ideas and aha moments, even when you miss an opportunity to follow through. Heck, there have been days when all I could say at its end was, "Thank God I don't have to live this one again!" And that was what I authentically celebrated!

Here are counterculture things to celebrate (not an exhaustive list):

- Feeling your feelings, especially the ones that are hard for you. Allowing yourself to cry or get angry. Feeling joy for no reason. Surviving a moment of embarrassment or shame without dying (it didn't kill you after all). Feeling your fear instead of running away from it.
- Not having an answer. You've left space for answers to come. You let yourself be human.
- Taking a day off. Saying no to someone. Even if you felt guilty afterward. You're moving in the right direction
- Taking a risk, even if it failed. Celebrate your courage!

- Celebrate spending less time berating yourself. Dropping a shaming story quicker than you have before.
- Sometimes it's taken courage just to get out of bed and get dressed. Give yourself credit for that.

This means not comparing yourself to what others are doing. That's beside the point. Celebrate you. We all need a gentler internal voice.

And by all means, welcome others into the culture of celebration you are creating. And know that not everybody gets to come into the sacred inner places. If they cannot support you in the culture you are building, they probably should remain outside in the courtyard rather than get a seat at the table next to you. When your culture is well established, it will spread outward. But make sure it's solid before taking it on the road day in and day out, trying to get others on the bandwagon.

2 Make yourself a priority.

"Put your own oxygen mask on first." If you've ever listened to the flight attendants doing their safety talk, they explain that in the event of a loss of cabin pressure, oxygen masks will drop from the overhead compartment. If you're flying with young children, instructions are to *always* put your own oxygen mask on *first*. This ensures the safety of your child *best*. We are better able to successfully care for others when we've taken care of our own needs. When our well-being is a priority, we enter into the world with more stability and carry with us the abundance of well-being. This makes way more sense than trying to serve from a place of depletion or lack, which can infuse our giving with stress, resentment, and scarcity. The effect of all we do and all we touch in the day will be different when coming from our own fullness. You'll feel it, and so will others. Rare will be the time of gritting your way through.

If you've come from the extreme of prioritizing others or even tasks over yourself, it will feel very strange and even uncomfortable.

You may not even know where or how to begin. And that becomes a great question to sit with in your journaling time! Answers always come. There is the promise of, "Seek and you will find, knock and the door will be open to you" (Luke 7:7 to quote the master teacher, Jesus). Don't be surprised if once you make the decision to begin to prioritize yourself, suddenly urgent obligations and responsibilities pop up. I see it happen again and again, in my own life, but also in the life of my clients. Hold steady and make yourself a priority. Let everything around you shift a little bit because it will. But you must *make* space for yourself. It's scary, but the time is now rather than later. In my experience, later never comes.

3 Don't dismiss the value of small beginnings.

They are infused with BIG intentions.

The answer to the question of, "How do you eat an elephant?" is, "One bite at a time." Begin right where you are; most often that's the current pain point in our lives. While idealistically we don't need pain to grow, it is often the very tool to our awakening, bringing bigger truths and revelations. And those revelations create more space for joy and ease. It certainly allows us to clear the clutter!

I'll finish with this.

It may get a bit messy as you learn and grow, but you can handle it. A big juicy life rich with all good things is worth a bit of mess. You've got this! And it sure beats the alternative!

For those who wish to enter a community of support, check out "Joy and Ease with Dawn Drew" on Facebook. I'd love to hear from you and have you join the conversation!

And for those who wish to go deeper, you can schedule a clarity call to see if one-on-one soul coaching is a good fit at joyandeasewithdawn@gmail.com or message me through "Joy and Ease with Dawn Drew" on Facebook.

And of course, I'm wishing you more joy and ease.

Additional Resources

While I've mentioned several throughout the book, I thought it may be helpful to just list them easily here along with some others you may find helpful. If you're not a book reader, many of these authors can be found on YouTube.

> *The Body Keeps the Score* by Bessel Van der Kolk
> *When the Body Says No* by Dr. Gabor Maté
> *Women's Bodies Women's Wisdom* by Dr. Christiane Northrup
> *Burnout: The Secret of Unlocking the Stress Cycle* by Emily Nagasaki, PhD, and Amelia Nagasaki, DMA
> *The Soul of Money: Transforming Your Relationship with Money and Life* by Lynne Twist

About the Author

Dawn Drew is a successful business owner and entrepreneur, and she is an empath and intuitive, an unlikely combination in the world of business. Straddling two worlds, that of business and spirituality, she's had to dig deep to find a rhythm of life that allows her to show up authentically in a world that doesn't always value heart-centeredness and, what she laughingly calls, the "woo-woo." In embracing both, she's found her true superpowers, allowing her to create a life of richness and meaning. She now helps others do the same. As a soul coach, Dawn works with those looking for something other than the cookie-cutter advice often given out today. They are looking for answers that fit them. Her prophetic and intuitive gifts along with her great compassion mean her clients are seen, heard, supported, and given powerful, practical tools and support.

Her private motto, "How hard can it be," has led her into many interesting places personally and professionally, providing quite the breadth of life experiences. Dawn has been hailed as a channel marker, one who marks safe passage for others and shows the way forward. She is the recipient of RESA's Top Most Influential People 2020.

These days, Dawn is appearing on podcasts and speaking on her favorite topics—creating a life of joy and ease: where to begin, shifting people-pleasing, and changing the work-earn-deserve mindset.

She is also the proud mother of four amazing kids, whom she calls her greatest teachers.

Printed in the USA
CPSIA information can be obtained
at www.ICGtesting.com
LVHW020838290224
773140LV00008B/171/J